Why Welfare States Persist

STUDIES IN COMMUNICATION, MEDIA, AND PUBLIC OPINION

A series edited by Susan Herbst and Benjamin I. Page

Why Welfare States Persist

*The Importance of Public Opinion
in Democracies*

CLEM BROOKS AND JEFF MANZA

THE UNIVERSITY OF CHICAGO PRESS   CHICAGO AND LONDON

CLEM BROOKS is the James H. Rudy Professor of Sociology at Indiana University.
JEFF MANZA is Professor of Sociology at New York University. They are the coauthors of
Social Cleavages and Political Change (1999).

The University of Chicago Press, Chicago 60637
The University of Chicago Press, Ltd., London
16 15 14 13 12 11 10 09 08 07   1 2 3 4 5

ISBN-13: 978-0-226-07583-9 (cloth)
ISBN-13: 978-0-226-07584-6 (paper)
ISBN-10: 0-226-07583-4 (cloth)
ISBN-10: 0-226-07584-2 (paper)

Library of Congress cataloging-in-Publication Data

Brooks, Clem.
  Why welfare states persist : the importance of public opinion in democracies / Clem
Brooks and Jeff Manza.
    p. cm.
  Includes bibliographical references and index.
  ISBN-13: 978-0-226-07583-9 (cloth : alk. paper)
  ISBN-13: 978-0-226-07584-6 (pbk. : alk. paper)
  ISBN-10: 0-226-07583-4 (cloth : alk. paper)
  ISBN-10: 0-226-07584-2 (pbk. : alk. paper)
  1. Welfare state—Public opinion.   I. Manza, Jeff.   II. Title.
  JC479.B76 2007
  320.51'3—dc22   2006030427

⊚ The paper used in this publication meets the minimum requirements of the American
National Standard for Information Sciences—Permanence of Paper for Printed Library
Materials, ANSI Z39.48-1992.

Contents

Figures and Tables

Figures

Tables

Acknowledgments

In writing this book we were fortunate to receive many generous comments and suggestions that strengthened and clarified our argument. We thank Elizabeth Armstrong, Jason Beckfield, Catherine Bolzendahl, David Brady, Paul Burstein, Edward Carmines, Jonas Edlund, Jeremy Freese, Theodore Gerber, Donald Green, Susan Herbst, Alexander Hicks, Nikole Hotchkiss, Michael Hout, Lane Kenworthy, Christian Larsen, Scott Long, John Levi Martin, Patricia McManus, John Myles, Ann Orloff, Benjamin Page, Devah Pager, Brian Powell, Rob Robinson, John Skrentny, Paul Sniderman, Brian Steensland, John Stephens, Robin Stryker, Stefan Svallfors, Timothy Tilton, Michael Wallerstein, Pamela Walters, Kim Weeden, and Christopher Wlezien. We presented parts of our work at the 2004 meetings of the American Political Science Association (Chicago), the 2004 meetings of the American Sociological Association (San Francisco), the 2005 meetings of the International Sociological Association's Research Committee 19 (Chicago), and in 2005 at the visiting fellows program in the Department of Sociology, Umeå University.

From the initial conceptualization of this project onward, Arthur Alderson provided us with detailed feedback, and we are pleased to acknowledge this debt. At the University of Chicago Press, we thank John Tryneski, and series editors Susan Herbst and Benjamin Page. Ben provided exceptionally constructive comments on two separate versions of the manuscript, for which we are especially grateful. Guidance and criticism supplied by two referees was invaluable. Our research was supported by a grant from the National Science Foundation (SES-0452873).

This project involved more than the usual amount of travel and time. Clem Brooks thanks the Department of Communication Science at the University of Amsterdam, where he was a visiting scholar in 2003–2004, colleagues at the Department of Sociology at Indiana University, and especially Ruth Kelly and Amanda and Lena Brooks-Kelly. Jeff Manza thanks his fellow scholars at the Russell Sage Foundation, where he was a visiting scholar in 2005–2006, Fay Lomax Cook and colleagues and staff at the Institute for Policy Research at Northwestern University, and especially Devah Pager and Dana and Zöe Hafter-Manza.

Introduction: The Welfare State, Mass Opinion, and Embedded Preferences

M odern welfare states shape both individuals' life chances and the level of inequality in a society. This conclusion, based on a generation of social science research, holds across developed democracies in North America, Western Europe, Australasia, and Japan. These countries are all *capitalist* democracies, characterized by the existence of private property and class inequalities. But at the beginning of the twenty-first century they are also *welfare* capitalist societies, making available a wide range of public provisions that include pensions, health care, unemployment benefits, child care, job training, and educational programs.

While providing support through social policies, however, contemporary welfare states differ in important ways. The extent to which private property and labor markets govern the life chances of individuals varies with the generosity of welfare state policies. In Scandinavia, for instance, governments provide an encompassing array of benefits and services to citizens, and this establishes a safety net from childhood through old age. Where social provision is lower, as in liberal-democratic regimes such as the United States, individuals rely more extensively on markets and other private sources of income. Pronounced differences between welfare states are key sources of the "varieties of capitalism" (Hall and Soskice 2001) that have animated recent scholarship in political economy and comparative politics.

The proposition that welfare states shape the patterning of inequalities in contemporary societies has a distinguished, if contentious, pedigree. In the wake of dramatic increases in postwar government spending in the United Kingdom, including the 1946 establishment of the National Health Service, T. H. Marshall (1950) advanced his seminal interpretation of the welfare state as the culmination of efforts since the eighteenth century to alleviate the class-based inequalities of industrial capitalism. In Marshall's account, the movement from "civil" to "political" and ultimately "social" citizenship was the hallmark of political modernization that would alter the very nature of market inequalities within Western democracies (see also Briggs 1961; Crosland 1964; Titmuss 1968).

The evolutionary scenario set forth in Marshall's writings stimulated a variety of reactions. These included endorsements by the pragmatic liberal architects of the welfare state such as Beveridge (1960 [1944]), as well as condemnation by libertarians who saw these developments as incompatible with individualism and the operation of free markets (Hayek 1994[1944]; see also Nozick 1974). Within the social democratic tradition, the establishment of modern welfare states was viewed as providing an opportunity to work toward an egalitarian vision of society (Crosland 1964), though this view was by no means universal. Indeed, many Marxists and left political theorists tended to dismiss welfare capitalism as anemic in the face of the class inequalities of twentieth-century capitalism (Marcuse 1964; Parkin 1971; Piven and Cloward 1971).

By the 1980s, however, the normative and economic failures of "actually-existing" socialism, combined with the growing generosity of welfare states (particularly in Western Europe), established welfare capitalism as an egalitarian alternative to free-market capitalism. Indeed, on the political right, recognition of the market-constraining impacts of welfare states prompted a new generation of critics (Murray 1994 [1984]; Mead 1986; Ohmae 1996). The growth of neoliberal doctrines was embodied in the governing ideologies of Margaret Thatcher, Ronald Reagan, and their followers around the world.

On the political left, the growing political momentum of free-market advocates in both domestic politics and global economic forums helped propel many skeptical commentators toward considerably more favorable views of welfare capitalism (e.g., Wright 1994; Piven and Cloward 1997). Defense of welfare state institutions subsequently became more than a reaction to shifting political currents. As we will see, a new generation of scholarship and political commentary on the welfare state has emerged, taking as its task analysis of the distinctive features and consequences of contemporary welfare states. The upshot of these intellectual and political trends is that the welfare state has come to occupy center stage in the politics of contemporary developed democracies.

Welfare State Effects on Poverty and Inequality

What is the evidence that welfare state policies have the consequences their proponents endorse and their critics fear? How significant is their impact? Can social policy interventions be effective in an era often said to be characterized by globalization and the dominance of multinational corporations?

Over the course of the past decade, a new wave of scholarship has analyzed cross-national data on individual and household outcomes, probing the linkage between welfare state generosity and inequality. The results point overwhelmingly toward the conclusion that high levels of welfare spending reduce both income inequality and poverty.[1] The magnitude of welfare state influence is considerable. One recent estimate (Moller et al. 2003) finds that a single point increase in welfare generosity lowers relative poverty rates by four percentage points. High levels of welfare spending raise, moreover, the well-being of such economically vulnerable groups as poor women and children (see Huber and Stephens 2000 and Conley and Springer 2001, respectively).

This recent scholarship provides striking confirmation for the long-held assumption that welfare states exert a fundamental influence over the nature of inequality within capitalist democracies. Indeed, it represents a fundamental advance over early sociological work on stratification in the postwar era that focused primarily, oftentimes exclusively, on individual or group-level processes in shaping stratification outcomes (e.g., Blau and Duncan 1967; Ganzeboom, Treiman, and Ultee 1991; see Grusky 2001 for review). This earlier scholarship implicitly discounted the impact of political institutions and public policies on stratification. The recent scholarship has set the record straight. It has vividly documented how government policies can reduce economic risks over the life course, lowering also the costs associated with such nontraditional family forms as single parenthood (McFate, Lawson, and Wilson 1995; DiPrete 2002; Gangl 2004). A full understanding of stratification systems requires examination not only of economic, social, and demographic factors, but also of the policy activities through which welfare states shape social inequalities.

The Political Foundation of Contemporary Welfare States

The centrality of welfare states to the patterning of inequality leads quite naturally to questions about the forces *behind* their emergence and on-going development. These issues have been the focus of a considerable body of research among political sociologists and comparative political scientists (Amenta, Bonastia, amd Caren 2001; Huber and Stephens 2001). Early welfare state scholarship argued for the importance of long-run industrial and economic trends that were common to twentieth-century industrial capitalism. Building from modernization theory, processes such as population aging and rising affluence were viewed as exerting pressures toward the emergence of the welfare state (e.g., Kerr, Dunlop, Harbinson, and Myer 1960; Cutright 1965; Wilensky 1975). While the first generation of welfare state scholarship offered important insights into economic and demographic sources of pressure on social policy emergence, it could not account for why countries later appeared to be taking varying developmental paths. Critics were also quick to question the lack of attention within the modernization tradition to the impact of political conflicts on social policy development.

A watershed in welfare state research was the appearance of the "power resources" approach in the 1980s (e.g., Korpi 1983, 1989; Esping-Andersen 1985, 1990; see also Stephens 1979). According to power resources theory, welfare states are a product of historical legacies of working-class power and left party influence over government. A key expectation is that welfare states tend to cluster into distinct "regime" types. Rather than the single type of welfare state envisioned by modernization theory, country- and region-specific patterns of political conflict and historical alliances lead to the establishment of distinct types of regimes (Esping-Andersen 1990). Scandinavian social democracies generally provide comprehensive benefits and services to all citizens, whereas the Christian democracies found throughout much of continental Western Europe balance high levels of government entitlement with the preservation of traditional (especially family) institutions. For their part, liberal policy regimes within the English-speaking democracies make more extensive use of the principle of means-testing in organizing and allocating government programs and services.

The analytical legacy of the power resources approach has been considerable. Its emphasis on cross-national variability has been an orienting theme for subsequent welfare state scholarship. To better appreciate the magnitude of cross-national differences in welfare states, consider Esping-Andersen's three ideal-typical regimes and data from the Organization for Economic Cooperation and Development. For 2001, these data reveal that welfare state spending constituted 27 percent of gross domestic product in social democratic countries. This overshadows the figure of 17 percent for liberal democracies.[2] At 26 percent of GDP, welfare spending in Christian democracies is also higher than in liberal democracies, and close to the figure for social democracies.

Cross-national differences of this magnitude demonstrate just how important it is to explain *why* such extensive variation exists. Complementing the power resources focus on class and partisan conflict, established welfare state theories have focused on political institutions, the legacies of past policies, and the political representation of organized interest groups. Advocates of different theoretical perspectives have engaged in vigorous debates over the past fifteen years, and we consider those perspectives in more detail in chapter 1.

But lying just below the surface of theoretical debates is the possibility that is central to this book; namely, that mass opinion is of consequence for social policymaking. In past work, numerous scholars have asserted with varying degrees of conviction the possibility that citizens' attitudes matter. But strikingly, there have been few analyses of the actual impact of public attitudes on welfare states. Clearly, one reason has been the absence until recently of truly comparable cross-national public-opinion data; most earlier attempts to examine the comparative impact of public opinion were based on surveys that were carried out at different times and used different measures of public preferences (Coughlin 1980). Though innovative for the time, these early investigations had a variety of methodological limitations to which critics continually returned (Weir, Orloff, and Skocpol 1988a; Skocpol 1992; Steinmo 1994). Reflecting, then, both the lack of suitable data and the sharp criticisms of early scholarship, welfare state researchers have been reluctant to incorporate mass opinion into theory and empirical research (Myles 2006).

To scholars unfamiliar with these research traditions, this state of affairs will likely seem perplexing. Most accounts of democratic politics contend that public policies reflect, albeit imperfectly and in a probabilistic fashion, the preferences of citizens (Burstein 1998; Manza and Cook 2002; see also Downs 1957). Given, for instance, extensive cross-national variation in aggregate welfare output, it is reasonable to ask whether higher levels of welfare state effort in social versus liberal democracies are explained by cross-national differences in mass policy preferences. Does mass opinion lie behind the operation of better-understood political mechanisms such as partisan control over government? Up to this point we have had little but hunches to guide our understanding.

We decided to write this book because we believe that questions about the social policy influence of mass opinion represent a central and constructive challenge for welfare state theory and research. Ignoring the policy preferences of national publics deprives scholars of a fuller understanding of the political foundations and trajectories of contemporary welfare states. Fortuitously, we now have both the data and the theoretical tools to systematically examine the question of mass opinion.

Our investigations build closely from an emerging literature on linkages between public opinion and public policy (Page and Shapiro 1983; Stimson, MacKuen and Erikson 1995; Erikson, MacKuen, and Stimson 2002a; see Manza, Cook, and Page [2002], and Burstein [2003] for overviews). "Policy responsiveness" scholarship has developed new research methods and theories for analyzing opinion/policy linkages. This research presents evidence for the influence of mass opinion over public policy outputs within the United States, the one country that has been most rigorously studied.[3] In doing so, the U.S. responsiveness literature provides an important source of additional motivation for investigating the possibility that mass opinion exerts influence over social policy within capitalist democracies.

American Exceptionalism?

Most research on policy responsiveness has focused on the United States. This is, of course, an intrinsically fascinating and important case. But it is also a country characterized by a combination of historical, political, and institutional attributes not found elsewhere. These include a majoritarian electoral system with no significant left (or religious) parties, weak unions, a decentralized polity coupled with extensive use of judicial review, and levels of public support for free enterprise that are high even among of the world's liberal democracies. Such attributes are clearly critical; they define what is distinctively "American" in comparison to other political systems. Yet we simply do not know how, and to what extent, these relatively unique features help or hinder policy responsiveness.

There is also considerable controversy among analysts as to the true level of American policy responsiveness. Is it high? Is it low? Or is it some-

where in between? Because the responsiveness literature lacks comparative evidence, there is no baseline against which to assess the magnitude
of policy responsiveness in the United States.[4]

Our investigation of linkages between mass opinion and welfare states
is useful in this context, bringing new results to bear on unresolved debates between scholars of American policy responsiveness. Whereas the
"strong" position on responsiveness provides a decidedly optimistic view
of citizens' ability to get their preferred policies (Stimson et al.1995; Wlezien 2004), a more "pessimistic" view is that elite influence and strategic
deception on the part of politicians sharply limit the operation of American democracy (see Domhoff 2002; Hacker and Pierson 2005). In bringing
the study of mass opinion to welfare state scholarship, we offer new results
for comparing American democracy to other democratic polities. This is an
important subsidiary goal of our investigation.

Embedded Preferences in Welfare States

In this book, we develop and consider the case for an *embedded preferences* approach to the politics of the welfare state. Our investigation highlights how, why, and to what extent mass policy preferences are an independent source of influence over welfare policies. We see two paths of influence. Elections provide an opportunity for voters to choose the government that enacts social policies. Yet the impact of mass opinion does not
stop there. Public support for (or opposition to) welfare state programs
may also influence the behavior of politicians once in office. A defining
feature of democratic polities is the likelihood of some degree of public
influence over the shape and direction of policymaking.

But policy preferences do not simply fall from the sky. Our theoretical approach also seeks to address questions concerning the origins of
citizens' policy preferences. This is where the "embeddedness" feature of
our argument comes into play. One popular view is that macroeconomic
factors are the key source of mass policy attitudes. Our own inclination is
to see policy preferences as grounded in a country's social structure, major
institutions, and the collective memory of citizens. Key social factors such
as religion, class, and education exert a far-reaching influence over how
individuals acquire and maintain (or relinquish) preferences concerning
matters of policy. *Who* people are matters considerably for what policy
attitudes they tend to adopt and maintain.

Borrowing from economic sociology, we use the term *embeddedness* to get at the social foundations of policy preferences.[5] Preferences concerning social welfare are not, we contend, merely an artifact of economic calculations and fluctuations in the business cycle. Welfare state preferences are organized by reference to the social relations and contexts in which individuals are situated. Citizens' identities, for example, as business managers, lone parents, or doctrinally conservative Christians matter to their policy attitudes.

Further, because the social factors behind preferences tend to change slowly over time, the embedded preferences approach provides a way of understanding the remarkable inertia that has tended to characterize attitudes toward the welfare state in many countries. This yields insights into how policy preferences have counteracted negative pressures on many contemporary welfare states. To anticipate one of our programmatic findings, cross-national differences between welfare states have proven robust in part because of deeply held citizen preferences, even in the face of massive changes in the global and economic environment in which governments and national publics are situated.

Developing the analyses with which to evaluate the embedded preferences approach is no small task. It requires us to conceptualize and measure policy preferences as a source of government activity within national and historical contexts that vary considerably. In addition to the use of an explicitly cross-national design, we must also devise a suitable measure of mass policy preferences. The analyses presented in this book combine updated data from the Organization for Economic Cooperation and Development with survey data from the International Social Survey Program. These merged data enable a systematic portrait of welfare states across countries and over time, bringing into explicit focus the key factor of policy preferences. Another challenge is to address statistical problems that are inherent in the analysis of country-level data. Our analyses draw upon and incorporate relevant innovations in cross-sectional time-series modeling.

Our argument is presented in seven chapters. In chapter 1 we begin by exploring how and why mass opinion has been largely absent in the major theoretical approaches to understanding welfare states. Of these approaches, power resources and path dependency theories *anticipate* a causal role for mass opinion. These approaches provide a key point of departure for our embedded preferences approach to the welfare state. Guided by the policy responsiveness literature, we consider the reasons why government officials have incentives to incorporate mass opinion into social policymaking above and beyond election outcomes.

In chapter 2, we present the first part of our empirical analysis. We begin by investigating whether differences in public policy preferences help to explain cross-national differences in welfare state regimes. We focus on social democratic, Christian democratic, and liberal regimes, with further results for comparing specific countries within and across the three major regime types. We find compelling evidence for the importance of mass policy preferences as a source of regime differences, even when we control for the demographic, political, and institutional factors established in previous research. This line of causal inference is further buttressed by results of our tests for reverse causation scenarios and other forms of endogeneity bias. Additional results show that while elections and the partisan composition of government mediate a portion of the effects of mass opinion on welfare state spending, a significant portion of this influence is direct. The influence of mass preferences is not confined to elections.

Chapter 3 extends the embedded preferences approach to controversies surrounding recent patterns of stability and change in welfare states. Increasingly, welfare states appear quite robust, yet their historical persistence within the turbulent global environment of the past two decades presents a challenge to scholars. Our embedded preferences approach suggests that a key part of the explanation lies with the constraining influence of mass policy preferences. As in chapter 2, our analyses control for established factors behind welfare states, and our results support a thematic conclusion: mass opinion is an important mechanism behind persistence tendencies in welfare states.

In chapter 4 we address a set of questions about the scenario of welfare state convergence. One argument for convergence has come from a vigorous reformulation of modernization theory, while a second concerns the European Union as a source of growing similarity among members' welfare states. Our analysis incorporates these claims, shedding light on pressures behind welfare state similarity versus difference during the past two decades. We find evidence for a modest degree of cross-national convergence, yet this phenomenon is a product of growing similarity *within* welfare state regime types, rather than all countries adopting the same model of social provision. Contrasting further with past theoretical arguments about convergence pressures, we find mass policy preferences to be central to the maintenance of current patterns of difference between countries and also regime types.

Chapter 5 shifts our focus from effects to *causes* of mass policy preferences. We consider two approaches to understanding the origins of such preferences. In the *economic* approach, mass policy preferences are shaped primarily by economic conditions, leading to a constantly cycling pattern of change in mass opinion. Our *embedded preferences* approach views policy preferences as having multiple social foundations that confer a degree of stability in the aggregate, resulting in the public's preferences changing slowly and in a more monotonic fashion. With reference to preferences concerning the welfare state, the analyses we present consistently favor our embedded preferences model, providing evidence against the capacity of economic factors to explain recent patterns of opinion change. Our discussion draws out implications for understanding the ways in which the social and institutional embeddedness of policy preferences contributes to inertia in the aggregate.

Much of our analyses focuses on the overall spending output of welfare states. This is appropriate in light of the centrality of expenditure to social policy effects on stratification. But an important set of further questions concerns the degree of responsiveness in overall versus domain-specific social policy outputs. We investigate these issues in detail in chapter 6. There, we consider a variety of domain-specific measures, including recent data on cash benefit entitlements. We find that government responsiveness generally is strongest with respect to overall welfare output, and there is also variation in the magnitude of policy responsiveness across specific domains such as old-age provisions and sickness benefits. These findings reinforce the importance of overall welfare output as a summary dimension of welfare states. They also suggest the likelihood that policymaking within specific domains is more heavily shaped by the influence of interest groups and strategic action on the part of politicians.

Our concluding discussion in chapter 7 returns to key implications for welfare state theory and research. We consider a number of possible challenges to our argument, reviewing the evidence and considering several issues in greater detail. We also explore implications of our results for debates concerning policy responsiveness in the United States. Responsiveness is not confined to the American case, for linkages between mass preferences and welfare state output are central to all developed democracies. Yet a core feature of U.S. politics currently is the market-oriented preferences of the American public. It is only from a cross-national perspective that this key feature of democratic variability comes into focus.

Where might recent developments influence the trajectories of welfare states in the near future? At the heart of our embedded preferences approach is the underlying possibility that changes in major institutions or alterations in the social contexts shaping mass opinion may transform the distribution of policy preferences within a society. The effects of such processes generally take some time to occur, and we develop a forecasting analysis to consider several scenarios through which policy preferences might experience a redirection. These include a scenario of demographic convergence as well as trends involving changing public views of the proper balance between states and markets. The results of our forecasts again attest to the multiple sources of welfare state policymaking, while also highlighting the potential of mass policy preferences to substantially alter the direction of social policy development.

CHAPTER ONE

Reaching for Mass Opinion

There is a surprising paradox in the intellectual history of research on the welfare state. There are numerous reasons—stemming from intuitive conceptions of how democracies operate as well as scholarly research on policy responsiveness—to expect that citizens' preferences will influence the extent and types of social provision that countries adopt. Indeed, some of the very earliest theorizing on the sources of welfare state variation pointed to differences in the "values" of national publics, and many leading contemporary analysts have identified public support for social spending as an important bulwark of the welfare state.

Yet remarkably, there have been few attempts to systematically assess or theorize the impact of mass opinion on social policy output. How can this be? Both theoretical assumptions and data limitations account for this state of affairs, and in this chapter we unravel the history of scholarly research on the foundations of welfare states and its curious neglect of mass opinion. Our account highlights the ways in which welfare state scholars have approached, in a variety of ways, the question of mass opinion without fully engaging it.

We begin with economic and functionalist theories of the welfare state advanced in the 1960s, and their more recent revival in the literature on globalization. These models emphasize welfare state convergence and reject the view that politics matters in the long-run trajectory of welfare state development. They can be contrasted with theories that emphasize the importance of political and institutional factors in producing cross-national variation in welfare states. In the last two decades, political models of the welfare state have been sometimes accompanied by invocations of public opinion as a source of welfare state persistence. But since 1980 there has been little examination of this underlying issue.

Our brief intellectual history sets the stage for the "embedded preferences" approach that we present and explore in the rest of the book. We
develop a theory of how mass opinion may shape social policy, as well as
a model of the sources of policy attitudes on the part of national publics.
Central to our argument is the idea that mass opinion undergirds the contemporary welfare state, providing in many countries a powerful source
of legitimacy its political defenders are able to draw upon. This is a notable phenomenon in the hostile climate of the late twentieth and early
twenty-first centuries, when forms of social provision established in earlier
decades have been under vigorous attack.

The Necessary Welfare State?

The Logic of Industrialism Thesis

Modern welfare states first emerged in societies experiencing rapid industrialization and economic growth, and the accompanying social problems
these developments generated. Much of the early scholarship on the welfare state took as its point of departure the assumption that economic development was a necessary precondition for the emergence of government
solutions to the inequities of industrial societies. Two distinct versions of
this thesis can be identified: a modernization version and a Marxist version.
The former—developed in the 1960s and 1970s—came to be referred to as
the "logic of industrialism" thesis (e.g., Kerr et al. 1960; Wilensky 1965,
1975; Flora and Alber 1981).

The logic of industrialism's central contention was that growing affluence provides the surplus as well as the stimulus for government to fund
new policy initiatives involving pensions, health care, and unemployment
insurance (Cutright 1965, 1967). Fueled by social, technical, and medical
advances that led to increased longevity, the aging of populations was further seen as exerting pressure on governments to address the needs of the
growing number of elderly citizens (Wilensky 1975; see also Pampel and
Williamson 1985, 1988). Public social provision in the logic of industrialism
model was sometimes identified as one of the "functional prerequisites" of
industrial capitalist democracies (Cutright 1965:537). In the most extreme
formulations, political conflicts or pressures were seen as largely irrelevant; as Wilensky (1975:xiii) put it in an oft-quoted formulation, "economic growth and its demographic and bureaucratic outcomes are the root
causes of the general emergence of the welfare state."

The logic of industrialism model was part of a larger scholarly paradigm that viewed modernization as the path common to all societies undergoing a transition from agrarian to industrial capitalism (Rostow 1960; Parsons 1960, 1971). These theories had a decidedly optimistic view of the social implications of modernization. They hypothesized that changes in the economy and class structure would provide individuals with continually expanding opportunities for social mobility (Kerr et al. 1960; Galbraith 1985[1971]). Economic development was seen as bringing about cross-national convergence, and enlarged social provision would take care of remaining social problems. In the long run, the political ideologies of particular governments were of far less significance in comparison to macro-economic and demographic forces promoting modernization.

T. H. Marshall's (1950) influential writings on the evolution of citizenship provided an important, if distinct, impetus behind the optimism of modernization theorizing. For Marshall, the evolution of citizenship involved a progression from the establishment of civil rights to both political rights (including the extension of the franchise) and ultimately *social rights* (that is, a right to an adequate standard of living). All societies were seen as passing through these stages. To be sure, Marshall did acknowledge persisting conflicts between the market and the social rights of citizenship produced by the rise of the welfare state, a point sometimes lost on later commentators. But his overarching thesis was that trends toward a more inclusive citizenship grounded in welfare states were the hallmark of modern industrial societies.

This steady evolution of social citizenship rights led, in turn, to an expectation of a largely homogeneous welfare state. This expectation was, in practice, indistinguishable from the logic of industrialism model's prediction concerning the emergence of social policy. Because both strains of theorizing viewed welfare states as varying little within industrial capitalism, they would be vulnerable to evidence concerning the diversity of social policy across countries.

Radical Theories of the Welfare State

While modernization theories suggested steady improvements in the well-being of individuals and families, neo-Marxist and other radical theories that appeared in the same era drew different conclusions. But on key points their logic was strikingly similar to the modernization paradigm. As noted by Myles (1984:93), radical theories of the welfare state sometimes adopted a "logic of capitalism" model that largely substitutes "capitalism" for "industrialization." Where the logic of industrialism thesis posited that industrialization generates social problems necessitating welfare state institutions, the "logic of capitalism" position is that market capitalism generates crisis tendencies and surplus workers, which welfare states are required to ameliorate and placate, respectively.

In O'Connor's (1973) famous formulation, the welfare state arises because of the need for the capitalist state to manage the "contradictions" between accumulation and legitimation, with social provision facilitating legitimation. The result is an inevitable "fiscal crisis" of the state. In other variants, social provision reflects a response to class struggles: in order to avoid the threat of pressure from below, elites occasionally are forced to make concessions to subordinate classes (Piven and Cloward 1971; Block 1977; Przeworski 1985).

In one important respect, however, radical theories did go beyond logic of industrialism approaches to consider a role for mass political consciousness. This can be seen most obviously in the Gramscian tradition within Marxism, where the securing of popular support for capitalism is a central explanatory problem. But other variations of radical political thought explicitly incorporated a role for political consciousness.

Class-struggle explanations pay close attention to the conditions under which the poor will revolt. And notwithstanding its structural-functional apparatus, O'Connor's account of the coming fiscal crisis of capitalist states emphasized the need for such states to secure popular support ("legitimacy") among workers for capitalism. In explaining the adoption of old-age pensions, for example, he proposed that

> the primary purpose of the system is to create a sense of economic security within the ranks of employed workers . . . and thereby raise morale and reinforce discipline. This contributes to harmonious management-labor relations which are indispensable to capital accumulation and the growth of production. (O'Connor 1973:138)

Other radical accounts of working-class opposition to capitalism grounded in the analysis of class struggles highlighted the centrality of "class consciousness." This too leads in the direction of considering public opinion; as Stephens (1979:71) once put it, "public opinion is nothing but a reflection of class consciousness, which is in turn a product of definite social forces, one of which is the level of labor organization."

Critical Assessments

As functionalist explanations of social phenomena have been subjected to methodological scrutiny by several generations of scholars (e.g., Homans 1964; Elster 1989; Cook 2000), the analytical limitations of both modernization approaches and radical theories have become apparent. Accounting for the timing and cross-national variation of welfare state development has been viewed as especially problematic (Orloff 1993b:42–50). The age distribution of the population and the level of economic development could not, by themselves, account for cross-national and historical differences in social program development and welfare state output.

Neo-Marxist and other radical theories of the welfare state suffer from a number of the same limitations, for these traditions move readily toward an undifferentiated conception of "capitalist" societies. Functionalist accounts of the reproduction "needs" of the capitalist system generating pressures for social provision are quite close to the logic of industrialism approach. Unless class conflict is reconceptualized as involving country- and time-specific contingencies (as in Piven and Cloward 1971 and Block 1977, or in the later power resources formulation), structural-functional approaches to class analysis provide an unsatisfactory perspective from which to explain the comparative development of welfare states.

Economic Theories of Globalization and the Welfare State

In spite of these problems, the idea that the welfare state is largely a product of, and shaped by, economic forces has been recently revived in the extensive literature on economic globalization. Globalization arguments have been marshaled to anticipate negative trends in contemporary welfare state development (e.g., Misra 1999; Rodrik 1997; Gilbert 2002). Here, the growing international mobility of capital is viewed as inducing "race to the bottom" pressures among governments seeking to maintain international competitiveness and avoid disinvestment.

Some analysts have advanced even stronger claims. One such contention is that economic globalization imperils the very idea of national sovereignty (Ohmae 1996; Boswell and Chase-Dunn 1999; Standing 1999). This would likewise constrain the ability of welfare states within specific countries to engage in public spending at rates higher than globally dominant countries such as the United States. In limiting the policy options available to national governments, economic globalization appears to set in place substantial incentive for policymakers to turn away from traditional forms of social provision (Greve 1996; Montanari 2001).

The literature on economic globalization has not been without controversy (for overviews, see Rhodes 1996; Berger 2000). Indeed, twenty years into its development, evidence for strong globalization impacts on social policy is notably problematic. Using established measures of welfare state output, economic globalization's core dimension of foreign direct investment can at best be said to have yielded a modest and occasionally *positive* influence (Iversen and Cusack 2000; Iversen 2001; Brady, Beckfield, and Seeleib-Kaiser 2005).

These results fit well, in retrospect, with a seminal line of commentary on issues of globalization and national sovereignty. According to this perspective, individual nation-states, particularly small polities whose economies have always depended upon high levels of trade and participation in the world economy, adjusted continuously in the post–WW II era to anticipate the uncertainties associated with globalization (Katzenstein 1985; Garrett 1998; Hall and Soskice 2001). Furthermore, welfare state policies such as jobs training programs and family services *enhance* economic productivity, rather than undermining a country's tax base. Social policy innovations within many European nations can be viewed as a bulwark against deindustrialization and related economic effects of the world economy (Iversen 2001). Recent patterns of economic globalization thus appear quite compatible with the maintenance of contemporary welfare states.

Moving beyond Economic Theories of the Welfare State

There are good reasons to be skeptical about economically reductionistic approaches to welfare states that leave little explanatory room for political factors. These theories have difficulty grasping extensive variation between countries and accounting for causal processes preventing "race to the bottom" tendencies. Taking these shortcomings as their point of departure, welfare state theories have introduced context-varying political factors into explanations of the development of public social provision. As we will see, these approaches, particularly in recent formulations, provide a springboard for considering the policy influence of mass opinion.

Political Theories of the Welfare State

National Values

It is striking that one of the early challenges to logic of industrialism and
Marxist approaches highlighted differences in welfare policy rooted in
"national" or "cultural" values (Rimlinger 1971; Coughlin 1980; Guest
1991[1980]; see also Lipset 1963, 1996). In this tradition, cross-national
variation in values was seen as providing the basis for different national
approaches to social provision. Societies with higher levels of support for
egalitarianism were viewed as far more likely than those with more individualistic traditions to build extensive welfare states (Rimlinger 1961,
1971; Lipset 1963; Coughlin 1980).

The national values thesis finds its most famous embodiment in theories of "American exceptionalism" (e.g., Lipset 1963). Americans were
portrayed in these accounts as having a distinct set of cultural values in
comparison to Europeans, stemming from the absence of a feudal past,
a putative openness of social structure, and the relative absence of class
consciousness. As a result, Americans were said to have rejected socialism
and other collective solutions to social problems. Only an unusual external
shock such as the Great Depression could partially overcome deep-seated,
individualistic values. As European democracies proceeded to build extensive welfare systems during the postwar era, the comparatively stingy
nature of the American welfare state could, then, be cited as indicative of
the power of liberal values in the United States (Lipset 1996).

But the early national values arguments had a number of limitations
that made them a relatively easy target for subsequent critics (e.g., Skocpol
1992: 15–23; Orloff 1993a; Steinmo 1994). From the standpoint of contemporary social science, the early national values scholarship lacked adequate microfoundations and a rigorous evidentiary base. Researchers simply could not access suitable cross-national data with which to test their
hypotheses. Indeed, at the time that national values analysts were writing, there were virtually no comparative survey data with standardized instrumentation, and the measurement of welfare state output was similarly
underdeveloped.

Critics of the national values approach argued that a static conceptualization of values made the latter a poor device with which to understand
the comparative and historical development of social insurance programs
(Skocpol 1992). Because national values, according to one prominent interpretation, were viewed as established by national and industrial revo-

lutions (Lipset 1963), their assumed stability made it difficult to explain patterns of policy change. A further criticism concerned analytical vagueness in the causal mechanism at hand. Was the "values" factor operating at the level of political elites, major institutions, the media, or ordinary citizens?

So vigorously were these criticisms expressed that they have at times been seen as undermining the validity of *any* welfare state explanation that considers mass opinion as an input into welfare state policymaking (Steinmo 1994; Immergut 1998; Thelen 1999). Yet this conclusion is unwarranted. As we discuss in detail later in this chapter, more recent public opinion theory and research provides the specificity and microfoundations that critics found lacking in the earlier national values models. Further, rather than banning all reference to mass opinion, the analytical logic of the most influential contemporary welfare state theories *anticipate* a causal role for mass policy preferences. It is to these theoretical approaches and their implications that we now turn.

Power Resources Theory

The inability of early theories of the welfare state, such as the logic of industrialism, to incorporate political factors in the making of welfare states provided a key point of departure for "power resources" scholarship (see Korpi 1983, 1989; Esping-Andersen 1990). This approach starts from the assumption that unequal economic relationships, particularly as exemplified in the class structure, facilitate the formation of social groups with distinct and competing interests. Within capitalist democracies, elections provide classes and class-related organizations such as unions with a recurring set of opportunities to extract benefits from national government, yielding policy influence on such issues as the length of the workweek or the extent of unemployment insurance. Class conflict—the "democratic class struggle," in Korpi's (1983) influential formulation—is thus a central mechanism in the development of welfare states.

Because the capacities of core classes such as industrial owners, farmers, and manual workers varies over time and across national context, the subsequent development of welfare states reflects the institutionalization of different patterns of class alliance. For instance, when a highly organized working class is successfully allied with farmers, this tends to facilitate the emergence of welfare states with extensive social provisions, as in the case of Sweden (Korpi 1983). There, universalistic social security programs were implemented in conjunction with price subsidies for farmers. By contrast, when the working class has high levels of regional or racial/ethnic fragmentation that inhibit class alliances, the interests of employers will figure more centrally in regime development, as in the case of the United States (Esping-Andersen 1990). Here, the provision of government services is considerably more restricted.

How do classes translate their collective interests into policy? Power resources theorists argue that the respective capacities of left, religious, or secular right-wing political parties are a key source of welfare state development (e.g., Huber et al. 1993; Hicks 1999). More specifically, the influence of political parties is said to operate in conjunction with the effects of class conflict, giving rise to party systems that bear the imprint of long-standing alliances between major classes and parties (Korpi 1989; Esping-Andersen 1990; Huber and Stephens 2001).

The proposition that nationally embedded conflicts involving social groups and political parties shape welfare state development suggests important conclusions about the variability of social policy. Rather than the single type of public policy system envisioned by Marxist or modernization theories, power resources analysts argue for the existence of different types of welfare state "regimes." In the most common such typology, there are three ideal types of welfare states: social democracies, Christian democracies, and liberal democracies (Esping-Andersen 1990; see also Castles and Mitchell 1993; Korpi and Palme 1998).

Power resources analysts see the four Scandinavian countries of Denmark, Finland, Norway, and Sweden as the core members of the *social democratic* regime type. In these regimes, governments provide high levels of benefits and services to all citizens, constraining the influence of markets. By contrast, the *Christian-democratic* welfare states of continental Western Europe—these include Austria, Belgium, France, Italy, Germany, Switzerland, and the Netherlands—balance high levels of government entitlements with the preservation of traditional (especially family) institutions. This reflects both the ideological legacy and political power of religious parties within these nations.[1] Christian democracies tend to provide fewer services such as state-subsidized day care and active labor market policies in comparison to social democracies; lower rates of women's labor force participation are indicative of the persistence of traditional gender roles within these polities (Orloff 1993a; Huber and Stephens 2000).

Among the developed democracies, the third regime type is the *liberal democratic* regime. The English-speaking democracies (Australia, Canada, Ireland, New Zealand, the United Kingdom, and the United States) are characterized by the weakest institutionalization of social citizenship rights. Reliance on private provision of welfare is more extensive, and public policies do comparatively less to limit market-based inequalities among citizens. The implementation of government programs also tends to differ, as liberal democracies make more extensive use of the principle of means-testing in distributing services and benefits. The restriction of many sources of income supplements to a segment of the population that must officially "qualify" for benefits thus contrasts with the more universal provision within social democracies.

The classification of welfare states into regime types has been widely influential, and for good reason: such classifications provide a parsimonious means of capturing features of welfare state variation that have proven robust in subsequent scholarship. To be sure, there have been vigorous debates concerning the number and boundaries of such categories, and alternative schemes have been advanced (e.g., Castles and Mitchell 1993; Kangas 1994; Kersbergen 1999). But the threefold typology of regime types, developed most famously by Esping-Andersen (1990) in his landmark work *The Three Worlds of Welfare Capitalism*—remains by far the most common approach within the comparative welfare state literature (Arts and Gelissen 2002; Castles 2004).

The importance of regime types introduces a key expectation of power resources theory: once established, the central characteristics of welfare states will tend to endure over time (Esping-Andersen 1990). The notion that welfare states are subject to institutional persistence recalls the logic of industrialism's thesis that evolutionary processes exert a continual demand for public services. But instead of demographic and economic factors facilitating the emergence of welfare regimes, the power resources expectation is that welfare state development is governed by political legacies that operate within specific national contexts (Huber and Stephens 2001).

How do these political legacies influence welfare state development, particularly in the face of negative pressures associated with budgetary crisis or fiscal constraint? The thesis that welfare state development is shaped by class forces (such as unions or party-based coalitions involving workers, farmers, and the new middle class) has much to recommend it as an account of welfare state emergence. But it faces significant challenges in explaining contemporary patterns of welfare state persistence. The relative size of the working class and the organizational strength of labor unions have tended to decline in all capitalist democracies (Waller-stein and Western 2000). A number of social democratic and labor parties have also reduced by varying degrees their commitments to egalitarian social policies (Huber and Stephens 2001), while experiencing uneven re-sults and periodic electoral reversals in many countries during the past twenty-five years. Power resources scholars are well aware of such trends (e.g. Esping-Andersen 1996b), but nevertheless argue for the persistence of welfare states, despite a weakening in the key social and political forces that brought them into existence.

One possible answer to this puzzle is that the endurance of welfare states rests on their *cross-class* character (e.g., Esping-Andersen 1990). For instance, because they directly benefit from many welfare state programs, middle-class citizens may join with the labor movement and its working-class members to support generous welfare programs. According to Korpi and Palme (1998), the encompassing scope of public services within Scan-dinavian welfare states contributes to higher levels of legitimacy in com-parison to regimes organized around means-testing. Universalistic polities, by reducing zero-sum conflict between welfare recipients and nonrecipi-ents, secure high levels of both middle- *and* working-class support (Svall-fors 1995, 1997; Rothstein 1998, chap. 6).

This line of thinking seems promising, but it raises a further, pressing question. Explanations that cite class-based coalitions must account for *why* such alliances arise and endure over time. It is not enough, for exam-ple, to know that manual workers and salaried professionals constitute a "cross-class" coalition. It is also necessary to explain why such a coalition exists or proves historically durable. Reference to working- and middle-class interests per se provides no explanation, because these interests are, by assumption, distinct or even divergent. To express this problem another way, the cross-class thesis simply raises the prior question of why members of different classes come to see their interests as converging on support for a generous welfare state in the first place.

Where does this leave power resource theorists when it comes to ac-counting for welfare state persistence? The most compelling answer, we would argue, ultimately leads to the preferences of mass publics. Power resources theorists have not systematically incorporated public opinion in accounting for welfare state persistence (but cf. Rothstein 1998: chap. 6). However, clear hints of a role for mass opinion as a source of policy inertia and persistence can be found in a number of recent statements.

With reference to factors linking partisan governance to policy output, for example, Huber and Stephens (2001:322) propose that mass opinion may operate as a "ratchet," whereby "the rapid growth of support for welfare state policies . . . that benefit a large portion of the population . . . then turns these policies into the new point of reference for discussions on further welfare state development." Korpi (2003:598) likewise suggests that "it can be argued that major welfare-state institutions are likely to be of relevance for the formation of values, attitudes, and interest among citizens in ways that are of relevance for patterns of collective action." On the persistence of welfare states, Esping-Andersen (2000:4) contends that "the ways in which welfare states have responded, so far, reflect mainly a logic of voter allegiance to accustomed benefits."

Such comments suggest that influential analysts in the power resources tradition acknowledge a causal role for public opinion in shaping social policymaking. In doing so, they propel power resources theories in an important direction, one in which questions concerning mass opinion can be forcefully articulated. The next step is to develop a theoretical model linking public opinion to welfare state output, as a necessary prelude to developing empirical evidence.

Political Institutionalism and the Welfare State

Power resources theorists have often made reference to the role of political institutions in shaping the institutionalization of class and other social cleavages within party systems (e.g., Esping-Andersen 1996a; Korpi and Palme 1998; Rothstein 1998). But although institutional concepts figure within the power resources model, they lie at the very center of "new institutionalist" models of the welfare state. In early "state-centered" statements within this tradition (Evans, Rueschemeyer, and Skocpol 1985), scholars made two arguments. First, state managers were hypothesized as having the capacities and at times opportunity to play key roles in the establishment or consolidation of welfare state institutions (e.g., Heclo 1974). Further, the structure of political institutions within a polity was seen as shaping the range of policy options and strategies operating in the development of welfare state programs (Weir, Orloff, and Skocpol 1988a, b). Electoral systems based on proportional representation have been viewed as facilitating welfare generosity (Alesina and Glaesar 2004).

Contemporary institutional analysts identify the constitutional design of governments as critical to welfare state development (see Immergut 1992; Swank 2002). In particular, polities that are characterized by high levels of decentralization are viewed as *lowering* the likelihood of generous or universalistic benefits programs; this is because the multiple veto points around which decentralized polities are organized provide opportunities for business organizations and their conservative political allies to block egalitarian policy initiatives. At the other end of the cross-national spectrum are polities whose institutions facilitate greater centralization and thus provide fewer opportunities for veto power. Centralized polities are said to be more inclusive, giving greater weight to a variety of voters and citizen groups, and reducing the otherwise disproportionate influence of high-resource groups in the policy-making process.

The level of institutionally defined veto points tends to cluster within specific groups of countries. Countries such as the United States and Canada are characterized by similar institutional characteristics, including the use of judicial review and single-member (plurality) districts, facilitating decentralization. In contrast, the high-spending welfare states within Scandinavia tend to exhibit considerably more centralization. It is this type of variation that political-institutional scholars see as particularly relevant to understanding cross-national differences in social policymaking. Moreover, while scholars within this theoretical tradition acknowledge the historical importance of noninstitutional factors in generating initial pressure for specific features of constitutional design (Katzenstein 1985; Hall and Taylor 1996), these features, once established, are extremely difficult to change. They operate as independent sources of influence over welfare states and public policymaking.

Initially, the political-institutional emphasis on state capacities and constitutional structures suggests little room for mass opinion. And indeed, some political institutionalists have deliberately sought to draw a sharp contrast between institutional approaches and those giving emphasis to public opinion (e.g., Heclo 1974:288–93; Skocpol 1992:15–23; Steinmo 1994). But it is also possible to discern a quite different interpretation of the role of mass opinion, as a mediator that translates institutional structures into a tangible form that politicians can "read."[2] According to this argument, political-institutional development shapes the policy preferences of voters, which may in turn facilitate the reproduction of a specific political system.

Path Dependency

A distinct and increasingly influential variant of new instititutionalist models of the welfare state emphasizes the operation of "path-dependent" processes in accounting for welfare state growth and cross-national variation. At the heart of the path dependency thesis is a simple but compelling insight: early developments in the history of social policy set nations on "paths" that, once adopted, are difficult to reverse (Pierson 2000; Hacker 2002). Established institutional arrangements, such as the degree of administrative centralization, electoral laws, or the scope of judicial review, are quite resistant to change and create incentives (and disincentives) for specific kinds of political behavior. A classic example of this kind of persistence can be found in the case of the QWERTY keyboard. Although illogical from the standpoint of maximal typing efficiency, it has proven impossible to dislodge (David 1985). This stems not only from the considerable costs of moving to an alternative data-entry system, but also from the familiarity and legitimacy that the QWERTY keyboard has itself come to acquire over time.

Complementing the influence of political institutions, path dependency scholarship identifies a second type of causal mechanism. Here, the key process is *policy feedback,* whereby the establishment of a new government policy itself exerts an influence over sources of welfare state support and the strategies of actors seeking to shape policy (Pierson 1993, 1994; Skocpol 1995). In elaborating the idea that "policy causes politics," Pierson (1994, 1996, 2000) has argued that self-generating tendencies operate within welfare states. Constituencies and expectations are created around policies that make them difficult to eliminate once they have been set in place.

Recent work on path dependency by Pierson (1996, 2001b) has proposed that the "old politics of welfare states," involving class and other historical factors that generated the initial demands for public social provision, have largely been displaced. The contemporary era of welfare state development is said to reflect a "new politics" characterized by novel constituencies and quite different incentives for expanding versus reducing government benefits and services. Policies such as pensions and health insurance have created new patterns of interest among program beneficiaries, providing incentives for government officials to maintain such policies. Public opinion can play a role in this process because, as Pierson (1996:176) has proposed, "politicians are likely to pursue strategies that will not damage their chances for reelection."

Reaching for, But Not Grasping, Public Opinion

We have thus arrived at the key analytical watershed in comparative welfare state research. Analysts within multiple theoretical traditions have anticipated the possibility that mass opinion is a factor relevant to shap-

ing social policymaking, and perhaps in accounting for differences between countries. But none of these scholars has taken the next steps of
explicitly theorizing and attempting to measure its policy impact. Mass
opinion is, we contend, the great black box of contemporary welfare state
politics.

Why have scholars not proceeded to develop systematic accounts or
analyses of mass opinion? Undoubtedly, one central reason has been the
absence, until fairly recently, of suitable comparative data. Early work, as
we noted, struggled within the confines of country-specific surveys to develop a portrait of cross-national differences in public attitudes toward
the welfare state (e.g., Lipset 1963; Rimlinger 1971; Coughlin 1980). But
the initial results they offered were thus vulnerable to methodological cri-
tiques or outright dismissal by skeptics. Analysis of linkages to policy outcomes was also absent in these largely descriptive studies, enabling skeptics to question whether mass opinion was truly the causal factor at work
in cross-national comparisons.

A second consideration has been a more general disinclination among
a number of scholars to allow for the possibility that the attitudes of ordinary citizens might influence the policymaking process (Burstein 1998).
"Critical" theories of public opinion have, for instance, questioned the coherence or very existence of mass opinion. In this view, "public opinion surveys present only a rough idea of what people generally think because the
results are highly sensitive to a number of factors . . ." (Domhoff 1998:172;
see also Bourdieu 1979). Following early commentary by Blumer (1948),
critical theorists have further argued that conventional measures of attitudes mask more dynamic forms of preference or identity that are "acti-
vated" in social movements and other mobilizing contexts (Herbst 1993;
Eliasoph 1998).

But critical theories have at best ambiguous implications for understanding the relationship between public opinion (as measured in polls
and surveys) and policymaking. They often fail to grasp how mass opinion
scholarship has addressed such challenges. Even assuming, *arguendo,* that
surveys create rather than measure public opinion, it is nonetheless possible that policy and political outcomes are still shaped by policymakers'
perceptions of public opinion based on those very polls.[3] Moreover, critical
theory's focus on the possibility of alternative opinions under historically
exceptional or hypothetical conditions, while of possible relevance to normative theory, entirely misses *empirical* questions about actually existing
levels of mass opinion and their linkages to policy outcomes.

The critical theory view of mass opinion is, moreover, flawed as an account of the incoherence or excessive malleability of aggregate mass opinion. Results of several decades' worth of research support instead a portrait of mass opinion as more responsive to historical and long-term factors than elite influence in such forms as campaign communication and political advertising. That mass opinion tends to display notably coherent patterns of change is informative, casting doubt on assumptions about its whimsicality on volatility (Page and Shapiro 1992). At the center of analytical progress in understanding these features of mass opinion are insights into how statistical aggregation filters out randomness or instability in estimates of mass attitudes (Stimson 2004). We turn to these considerations as part of our larger theorization of the social policy influence of mass opinion.

Embedded Preferences and Welfare States

Public preferences are a hitherto residual mechanism behind the development and persistence of welfare state institutions. The questions to be asked are, Under what conditions do these preferences influence policy outputs? And how are welfare state preferences organized with respect to the relations and institutions of a society? The existing literature on policy responsiveness provides a useful point of departure.

Social Policy Responsiveness

In democratic polities, elected officials have an incentive to incorporate the policy preferences of voters so as to reduce the risk of electoral losses for themselves (or for members of their party), and also reduce the possibility of public reprisals in the form of civil disobedience or protests. The *policy responsiveness* proposition has been a key analytical innovation within the emerging tradition of opinion/policy research (Stimson 1995; Burstein 1998; Erikson et al. 2002a, b; see also Page and Shapiro 1983). It provides a missing link between the policy preferences of citizens and the distribution of incentives among government officials. We bring the policy responsiveness thesis to the study of welfare states to understand the foundations of linkage between mass opinion and social policymaking.

Of course, like any theoretical proposition, policy responsiveness may fail to accurately describe policy dynamics within specific historical and comparative settings. To date, opinion/policy studies have focused primarily on the case of the United States (for reviews, see Burstein 1998, 2003; Manza and Cook 2002; Wlezien 2004). Several innovative studies have also analyzed opinion/policy linkages within Canada and select European countries (Brooks 1990; Petry 1999; Soroka and Wlezien 2004, 2005). These studies have relied on measures of policy preferences (and government output) that are specific to individual countries, introducing uncertainty into subsequent estimates of opinion/policy linkages. But taken together, the U.S.-centered literature and its extensions to other polities provide a rich foundation for generalizing the study of opinion/policy linkages to comparative welfare state research.

We identify two central processes through which opinion/social policy linkages operate. The first is through a prior influence over the behavior of voters in elections. National elections provide a regularly occurring opportunity for the preferences of voters to influence government officials *indirectly*, provided such preferences can be used to evaluate parties and candidates.[4] The best comparative evidence suggests that voters do, in fact, choose between parties in part on the basis of policy preferences (e.g., Heath et al. 1991; Knutsen 1995; Dalton 1996; Alvarez and Nagler 1998). Voters' preferences on policy matters can be expected to influence the output of welfare states indirectly by affecting who is elected to office in the first place.

But mass opinion also exerts a *direct* influence over governments and welfare states. A key reason for direct policy responsiveness is that political incumbents and government officials have a strong incentive to avoid electoral sanctions and such other indications of voter disapproval as mass protests (Burstein 1999; McAdam and Su 2002). Politicians tend accordingly to anticipate and incorporate mass opinion *prior* to an actual election (Erikson et al. 2002a; Wlezien 2004). But for politicians and policymakers to have sufficient reason to respond in this fashion, three conditions must be met: first, mass opinion must concern issues of relevance to choices between competing policy options; second, the signal sent by mass opinion must be coherent and give little indication of randomness or instability; and third, the attitudes in question must reflect some non-zero degree of salience among the public.

What issues meet these qualifications? First, only a relatively small subset of citizens' attitudes in capitalist democracies are of relevance to public policymaking. The scope of mass public opinion is virtually limitless, for citizens have views about such things as mystery novels and the existence of unidentified flying objects. But issues of this sort are of limited relevance to government officials and welfare states. They map poorly onto the policy agendas of national legislatures and major political parties.

But matters such as pensions or health care are different. These represent a window into programmatic conflicts about the degree to which a society should be organized around government versus individual responsibility for social problems. Within capitalist democracies, competing views of social welfare among political parties, interest groups, and ordinary citizens represent a central cleavage (Taylor-Gooby 1993; Garrett 1998; Hicks 1999), with countries differing according to whether public policies give greater priority to government or instead to private forms of social provision.

By virtue of this political centrality, citizens' preferences regarding welfare state provision meet the three conditions necessary for direct influence on policymaking. Variation in mass policy preferences within a country generally correspond to competing positions endorsed by political parties or interest groups. With respect to internal coherence, aggregate policy preferences suggest coherence as well as a pattern of stable, or, alternatively, monotonic trends (Page and Shapiro 1992). Further, countries can frequently be ranked according to their aggregate degree of welfare state support (Smith 1990b).

Given extensive cross-national variation in welfare state policy and spending activities (as we will see in chapter 2), we expect that generous welfare states in social democracies (and, to a lesser extent, Christian democracies) are organized by reference to citizens' preferences for public social provision. In contrast, smaller welfare states within the liberal democracies are buttressed by a greater preference for private alternatives. Evidence regarding cross-national differences in mass policy preferences (Smith 1987, 1990b; Shapiro and Young 1989; Kluegel and Miyano 1995) is in line with this expectation, and steady accumulation of comparative opinion data has brought these differences into clearer perspective. In general, welfare state support is higher in West European societies in comparison to the United States and other liberal democracies, and highest within Scandinavia (Martinussen 1993; Svallfors 1995; 1997; Andersen, Goul, Pettersen, Svallfors, and Uusitalo 1999; Blekesaune and Quadagno 2003).[5]

Where does this line of thinking lead? A key implication of our argument is that citizens' preferences for models of welfare lend legitimacy to specific trajectories of social policymaking, and, further, to the political parties and governing coalitions seeking to implement these visions. Within Scandinavian democracies, for instance, comparatively high levels of welfare support are a critical source of welfare state legitimacy. By contrast, when support is lower within countries such as the United States, mass policy preferences are a comparatively greater resource for parties and activists who endorse private models of social provision and tax cuts. Like high levels of organization among manual workers, public support for the welfare state is thus a left power resource. But mass policy preferences may have even *greater* salience within democracies because they involve the public as a whole, in contrast to pressures exerted by specific groups and organizations.

The Origins of Welfare States Preferences

If mass policy preferences are key to the diversity and persistence of welfare states, it is critical, in turn, to ask, What are the sources of these preferences? In providing answers to this question, we distinguish between two competing approaches in the study of mass attitudes. The first of these sees citizens' policy preferences as multicausal in origin, rooted in demographics, social identities, and institutional environments. Because of their socially embedded character, policy preferences are expected to have a degree of inertia and aggregate stability—hence our reference to the *embedded preferences* approach. In contrast, the *economic* model views mass policy preferences primarily as a product of individuals' economic calculations. This leads to expectations of greater volatility and cyclicality in aggregate opinion, coinciding with patterns of economic change.

In fleshing out our embedded preferences approach, we point to three types of causal mechanisms that give preferences their embedded character. The first of these is the interests individuals have by virtue of social-structural locations involving unequal access to, or possession of, resources (Lipset 1981; Manza and Brooks 1999; Iversen and Soskice 2001). A large body of survey-based evidence has documented the effects of social cleavages, including class, race, and gender on policy attitudes (e.g., Kinder and Sanders 1996; Brooks and Manza 1997), suggesting further a degree of historical and cross-national patterning in the influence of these factors. Because social structure changes slowly over time, individuals' locations within social cleavages such as class structure contribute to stability in aggregate policy preferences within a society.

A second type of causal mechanism behind policy attitudes relates to the discursive communities present within such major social institutions as churches, families, and schools (Erikson and Tedin 1995; Smith 1998). Regular participation within these institutions exposes individuals to dominant or challenger political cultures. This exposure disseminates, reinforces, and at times transforms individuals' policy preferences (Sherkat and Ellison 1997; Steensland et al. 2000). Like social cleavages, major institutions are generally quite stable over short periods of time, and this contributes to inertia in aggregate opinion. By the same token, institutional transformations can contribute to trends in mass opinion, as when, for instance, new patterns of religious practices or school instruction set in place a basis for aggregate opinion change through cohort replacement. While institutionally driven changes can take decades or longer to occur, their cumulative impacts can be powerful in contributing to trends in aggregate opinion, as suggested by notable cases of expansion in U.S. higher education and growing secularism within Western Europe (e.g., Nunn, Crockett, and Williams 1978; Wuthnow 1988; Smith 1990a; Warner 1993).

A third type of mechanism behind policy preferences relates to citizens' *collective memories* of welfare state development. Collective memory scholars have demonstrated how enduring views of state-making, where these are often stylized and characterized by strong emotional narratives, can profoundly shape the identity and behavior of major groups within a nation (e.g., Olick 2003; Zerubavel 2003; Eyerman 2004). The arguments of collective memory scholars readily generalize to social policy development. We expect that citizens' level of preference for public versus private social provision is influenced by historical narratives about the degree to which past efforts at developing welfare state institutions have proven successful. For instance, in line with recent commentaries on welfare state legitimacy (Korpi and Palme 1998; Rothstein 1998), the establishment of *universalistic* regimes foreshadows their high levels of subsequent popularity, for the collective memories that tend to arise within these regimes have been quite favorable in tone. In contrast, welfare states that are vulnerable to partisan criticism or retrenchment tend to elicit lower public support, because the narratives they have inspired are frequently more negative, invoking fewer symbols of national pride or necessity, while generating also higher levels of resentment of welfare recipients (Gilens 1999; Pierson 2001b).

Stepping back from consideration of specific types of causal mechanisms, a central feature of our embedded preferences approach is its intrinsically multicausal focus: mass policy preferences are governed not by a

single factor but rather by individuals' locations within multiple social relations and organizations, and also with reference to country-level processes
involving collective memories of state-making. This multicausal portrait
yields a thematic prediction about over-time trends in mass opinion: because policy preferences have multiple sources, short-term change in a
specific causal factor will tend to have limited or modest effects on aggregate opinion insofar as it will be muted by the simultaneous operation
of other factors. This means that unless a number of causal factors all operate to propel aggregate opinion in a consistent direction, welfare state
preferences within a country will tend to exhibit a degree of stability in
the aggregate, especially over a short-term period of several years or a
decade. Aggregate trends can be expected, but they will tend to unfold
over a longer period of time.

With respect to cross-national variation, causal factors operating within
specific countries often have complementary effects. In the United States,
for instance, the popularity of individualistic ideas about government coupled with a large middle class that relies extensively on private pension
supplements and employer-provided health insurance reinforces low levels of support for the welfare state. By contrast, greater dependence by
all citizens on public services coupled with positive collective memories of
social policy innovation generates stronger aggregate preference for the
welfare state in Sweden.

The assumptions underlying the embedded preferences approach provide a sharp contrast with the economic model of mass policy preferences
(Downs 1957). According to this approach, the policy preferences of the
public are a function of individuals' economic calculations of expected
utility. Positive economic expectations on the part of voters provide less
reason to prefer high levels of social spending. Negative economic expectations, stemming, for instance, from rising unemployment, dispose individuals to prefer greater government provision of jobs or income security.

Because economic factors can vary considerably over short periods of
time, the economic approach leads to a portrait of mass opinion as highly
changeable, even unstable, with the public's preferences adjusting constantly to recent economic or policy events (Stimson et al. 1995; Wlezien
1995). But this portrait of mass opinion generates a number of paradoxes
when applied to the study of welfare state attitudes. For instance, pro-
longed periods of economic uncertainty or even downturn do not appear
to have transformed policy preferences within countries such as Sweden
during the early 1990s or the United States during the 1970s. Furthermore,

setting aside questions about the effects of economic factors, it is not clear how the economic approach can explain away accumulated evidence that noneconomic factors such as social cleavages and religion influence the policy preferences of individuals. While considerations of this sort are in line with the embedded preferences approach, a more systematic adjudication of these models awaits presentation in chapter 5. For now, the key point is that both economic and embedded preferences approaches provide a plausible basis for expecting linkages between mass opinion and welfare state outputs.

Conclusion

In this chapter, we have examined how the most influential contemporary theories of the welfare state have invoked mass opinion, but not theorized its operation or empirically analyzed its policy impact. The metaphor we have employed to summarize existing scholarship—"reaching for mass opinion"—suggests an incomplete outcome, one that it is now time to rectify. We turn in the next five chapters to the empirical investigations that together begin to provide answers to questions about the impact of mass opinion on welfare states.

CHAPTER TWO

Do Policy Preferences Explain Welfare State Differences?

I n 2001, welfare state spending in the Scandinavian social democracies was 59 percent greater than in liberal democracies, and a stunning 80 percent greater than in the United States. These are enormous differences. Do mass policy preferences help to account for the wide variation among contemporary welfare states? That question is the focus of our investigation in this chapter.

An extensive pattern of cross-national variation is a central expectation of contemporary welfare state theories, as we saw in the last chapter. But whether the causal factors identified by these approaches can fully explain welfare state differences in the contemporary era—as opposed to accounting for how welfare states arose in the first place—is unclear. Our embedded preferences theory, spelled out in chapter 1, provides a potentially useful explanation for the paradox of large and persisting welfare state differences.

In this chapter, we bring this explanation to bear on the large differences between welfare state regimes. We also consider the contribution of mass policy preferences to understanding finer-grained differences between specific countries, taking into account established factors as well. These cross-national comparisons lay the foundation for the questions about time trends that we address in chapter 3.

Conceptualizing and Modeling Welfare State Output

What is the relationship between mass policy preferences and welfare states? Figure 2.1 provides an initial glance, using a new dataset that we have assembled from the Organization for Economic Cooperation and Development (OECD) and the International Social Survey Program (ISSP), which we will describe shortly. The figure suggests the existence of a strong opinion/social policy linkage, where greater preferences are associated with higher levels of welfare state generosity. A regression line from a bivariate model would fit quite well the cluster of observed data points. But this evidence is only preliminary: it does not yet consider the possibility that the relationship is confounded by other factors.

In order to test that question, we need analytical tools that will allow us to model mass policy preferences alongside the causal factors established by past welfare state research. We also need to explain how best to measure welfare state output. We now turn to that discussion.

A New Cross-National Dataset

Our investigations require high-quality data on both welfare state output and mass policy preferences from a suitably large number of countries. The data should be fully comparable across countries. Welfare state measures must be derived using standardized definitions of social policy activity. Data on mass policy preferences must be based on items that employ identical question wording and response formats across country-specific surveys. The latter requirement is especially important, yet it places sharp limits on what data are appropriate to the tasks at hand. It is only fairly recently that fully comparable cross-national surveys measuring social policy attitudes have accumulated enough countries and time periods to enable analysis. We take advantage of data from the ISSP.

The ISSP data are unique. Unlike the Eurobarometer and the European Social Survey series, the ISSP also surveys non-European democracies, including Australia, Canada, Japan, New Zealand, and the United States. The other major cross-national opinion survey, the World Values Survey, is much sparser when it comes to welfare state issues. The use of different item wordings also frustrates cross-national analysis in several countries/time periods. The importance of a *fully* comparative cross-national design is critical. Evidence from single-country studies is insufficient for evaluating whether mass policy preferences are a factor behind cross-national differences between welfare states. Moreover, estimates derived from analysis of data that are specific to individual countries cannot be directly compared. For instance, analyses of the effects of policy preferences on welfare state output in the United States and Sweden that

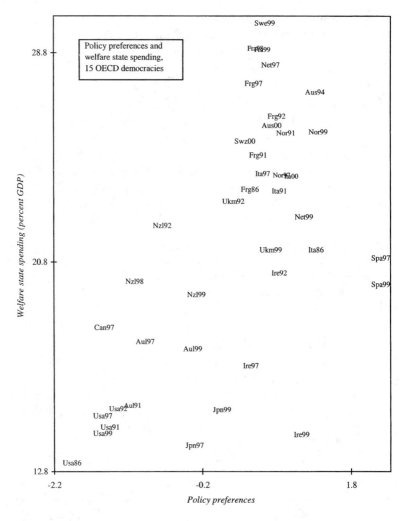

FIGURE 2.1. Interrelationship of policy preferences and welfare state output. Data are from the ISSP/OECD dataset.

are based on operational definitions or item wordings that vary between surveys fielded in particular countries introduce methodological artifacts. Absent cross-nationally standardized data, there are no means for ruling out such biases.

In this chapter and the remainder of the book, we analyze a new dataset that combines economic, demographic, and government spending data from the OECD, the ISSP, and the *Comparative Welfare States Dataset* (Huber et al. 2004). The OECD's careful use of consistent definitions and measures has made it the primary source of government spending data within welfare state research. To obtain measures of established factors behind welfare states, we extract data from the OECD's *National Accounts* (2003d), *Main Economic Indicators* (2003b), and *Labour Force Statistics* (2003a), supplemented with data on partisan governance and political institutions from the *Comparative Welfare States Dataset* (Huber et al. 2004). Data from the *Social Expenditures Database* (OECD 2005) are used to measure welfare state policy output. We use survey data from the ISSP's *Religion I, Religion II, Role of Government I, Role of Government II,* and *Role of Government III* surveys (International Social Survey Program 1988, 1993, 1994, 1999, 2001) to measure mass policy preferences over time and across countries.

We merge these data into a new country-level dataset containing measures of welfare state outputs and country-specific levels of mass policy preferences, as well as further measures incorporating the insights of previous welfare state research. Throughout the book—with the exception of chapter 5—the unit is the country-year. This country-level design is essential for conceptualizing *aggregate* opinion as an input into national policymaking (Page and Shapiro 1983; Stimson et al. 1995). As we discussed in chapter 1, it is aggregate rather than individual opinion that lies at the heart of questions concerning policy responsiveness. Individual-level data, by themselves, are not appropriate for analyzing opinion/policy linkages; it is only when they are aggregated that a suitable research design can be developed.

The dataset that we analyze in this chapter is composed of observations for sixteen developed democracies, and the historical era covered by these data is the period between 1986 and 1999. In all, there are forty-four country-observations for the liberal democracies of Australia,[1] Canada, Ireland, New Zealand, the United Kingdom, and the United States; Christian democracies are represented by observations for Austria, France, Germany, Italy, the Netherlands, Spain, and Switzerland, with Norway and Sweden as paradigmatic social democracies. Japan constitutes a further case. Low spending levels and the limited use of universalistic entitlements place the Japanese welfare state in closest proximity to liberal democracies, and we follow other recent analysis (Swank 2002) in classifying Japan as a liberal democracy. It should be noted that excluding Japan from the liberal ideal type has, however, little effect on subsequent results.

Welfare State Effort as the Dependent Variable

Comparative welfare state research has been heavily influenced by the concept of *welfare state effort,* measured as the ratio of total social spending to gross domestic product (GDP). Effort-related measures identify spending as the key output of welfare states, and placement of GDP in the denominator captures the idea that it is the extent of spending *relative* to a society's overall productivity that summarizes differences in welfare states over time and across national context. Effort measures were introduced in early quantitative studies of the welfare state (e.g., Wilensky 1975; Pampel and Williamson 1985), and they remain central to much contemporary scholarship (e.g., Pierson 1994; Huber and Stephens 2001; Castles 2004).[2] Because the OECD social expenditure measure includes both cash transfers and services, it captures the full range of public social provision.

Why is social spending effort a good measure of contemporary welfare states? First of all, there is an impressive body of empirical evidence that demonstrates how spending influences levels of poverty and inequality in the developed democracies (Kenworthy 1999; Huber and Stephens 2001; Brady 2003a; Moller et al. 2003). Spending measures capture the components of welfare states that are known to directly influence the contours of stratification. Further, because most earlier studies use similar or identical measures as their dependent variable, comparisons with previous research is facilitated. Finally, while much recent interest has centered on measures of replacement income within specific policy domains (Korpi 2003; Allan and Scruggs 2004; Scruggs 2004), indices of this sort are limited, even potentially biased, as measures of the *overall* output of welfare states. Replacement income measures tend to ignore the critical *service* dimension of welfare states (Huber and Stephens 2001). We discuss these limitations in chapter 3, providing further analyses and tests using replacement income measures.

Table 2.1 summarizes our welfare state measure, which consists of government expenditures on nine categories of cash and in-kind benefits and services *relative* to a country's GDP. In addition to spending outlays for the central domains of health care and pensions and services for the elderly, this measure includes social spending on smaller yet substantively important domains such as labor-market policies and family cash benefits and services. The inclusion of services is appropriate because of the importance of such programs for welfare states as a whole. The OECD measure of overall welfare spending effort provides a more accurate picture of the

TABLE 2.1 **Main Dependent Variable in the Analysis**

Variable	Description	Data Source
Overall welfare state effort[a]	Government expenditures on cash and in-kind benefits and services (9 categories)[b] as a percentage of GDP	OECD Social Expenditures Database (SOCX)

[a]Country-years in the analysis: Australia (1987, 1991, 1997, 1999), Austria (1994, 2000), Canada (1997), France (1998, 1999), Germany (1986, 1991, 1992, 1997, 1999), Ireland (1992, 1997, 1999), Italy (1986, 1991, 1997, 2000), Japan (1997, 1999), the Netherlands (1992, 1999), New Zealand (1992, 1998, 1999), Norway (1991, 1997, 1999), Spain (1997, 1999), Sweden (1997, 1999), Switzerland (2000), the United Kingdom (1991, 1992, 1999), and the United States (1986, 1991, 1992, 1997, 1999).
[b]Old-age benefits, survivor benefits, disability and sickness benefits, health services, family benefits and services, active labor market programs, unemployment benefits, housing, and residual provisions (including immigration policies).

magnitude of comparative and historical variation in welfare states, and the data we analyze are from the most recently updated *Social Expenditures Database* (OECD 2005).

The Measurement of Mass Policy Preferences

To measure mass policy preferences across countries and over time, we use data from five International Social Survey Program (ISSP) surveys (International Social Survey Program 1988, 1993, 1994, 1999, 2001) conducted between 1985 and 2000.[3] Care was taken by ISSP planners and principal investigators to field questions in a standardized way across different national contexts. The importance of the identical survey items in the ISSP is worth emphasizing. The effects of differences in question wording or response formats are problematic in social-scientific research, for they risk inaccurate estimates of both the true level of variables and their interrelationships with other measures. The topical focus of ISSP surveys on policy questions makes them an exceptional resource for welfare state and public opinion scholars.

We list at the bottom of table 2.2 the pair of survey items from which our measure of mass policy preferences is derived. These items ask respondents about their preferences regarding government responsibility for providing employment opportunities and for reducing income inequality, issues that are at the center of ideological and policy conflicts over welfare states. As summarized in the table, these two ISSP items scale with a high degree of reliability, and scores are for country-years. These items are drawn from a larger battery of questions about attitudes toward social policy. Analysis of this battery reveals that the pair of items in table 2.2

TABLE 2.2 **Independent Variables in the Analysis**

Variable	Description	Data Source
Economic factors		
Per capita GDP	Per capita gross domestic product in thousands US$ purchasing power parity-adjusted.	OECD National Accounts
Demographic factors		
Women's labor force participation	Female labor force participation as a percentage of female population age 15 to 64 years (coded with 1-year lag).	Comparative Welfare States Database (CWS), OECD National Accounts
Immigration rate	Net migration as a percentage of 1,000 population.	OECD Factbook
Political institutions		
Veto points	Scale of five measures of federalism (0–2), parliamentary vs. presidential system (0–1), strength of bicameralism (0–2), use of judicial review (0–1), and proportional representation (0–2).	CWS
Partisan control of government		
Religious party control	Percentage of seats held by government parties controlled by Christian-democratic and Catholic parties.	CWS, election statistics agencies, various years
Left party control	Percentage of seats held by government parties controlled by labor, social-democratic, socialist, and communist parties.	CWS, election statistics agencies, various years
Cumulative left party control	Cumulative left party percentage from 1946 to year of observation	CWS
Mass policy preferences		
Policy preferences	Scale[a] constructed from two survey items below (coded with 1-year lag): *On the whole, do you think it should be or should not be the government's responsibility to: Provide a job for everyone who wants one? On the whole, do you think it should or should not be the government's responsibility to: Reduce income differences between the rich and the poor?* 1. definitely should not be; 2. probably should not be; 3. probably should be; 4. definitely should be	International Social Survey Program Surveys 1985–1986, 1990, 1991, 1996, and 1998. Role of Government I, II, and III; Religion I and II

[a]$\alpha_{\text{reliability}} = .92$

accounts for just over 50 percent of the total variance, with the eigenvalue for the next largest component dropping considerably. The two items in question thus summarize well the underlying dimension of mass policy preferences that are measured by the larger set of ISSP items. This is important, because while the pair of items we use were fielded in five separate ISSP surveys, other items from the larger battery are available in only three surveys. This would severely limit the number of country-years available for time-series analysis. However, exclusion of these other items from our aggregated measure of policy preferences is of limited consequence in light of the factor-analytic results.

Following Page and Shapiro (1983) and Stimson et al. (1995), scores for mass policy preferences are lagged by one year. This captures the likelihood that public opinion influences the budgetary cycle of policymaking during the following year. In the multivariate analysis, country-specific observations for policy preferences at time $_{t-1}$ are paired with welfare state effort and other independent variables measured at time $_t$ (unless otherwise noted).

Mass Policy Preferences as a Source of Welfare State Policy

How, precisely, do policy preferences vary across types of welfare state regimes? In figure 2.2, we present data for the average level of policy preferences in social, Christian, and liberal democracies in 1996, with results for the United States providing a further point of comparison. In keeping with past cross-national studies of policy preferences (Smith 1987; Kluegel and Miyano 1995; Svallfors 1995, 1997; Andersen et al. 1999), welfare state support varies widely, and in a patterned way. Citizens in European democracies exhibit high levels of support, followed more distantly by individuals in liberal democracies, with Americans exhibiting the lowest level of preference for welfare state provision.

The magnitude of these differences merits further comment. The standard deviation for the three regime types (.76) is well over two-thirds the standard deviation for all countries (1.10). This means not only that policy preferences differ substantially across countries falling into the *same* regime type, but that between-regime differences also capture a substantial portion of the variability in preferences across *all* developed democracies. In other words, a good deal of the cross-national variability in social policy attitudes is a product of highly patterned differences between social, Christian, and liberal regime types.

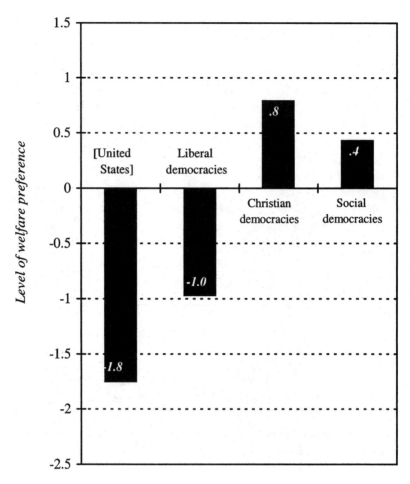

FIGURE 2.2. Policy preferences in social, Christian, and liberal democracies, 1996. Data are from the International Social Survey Program.

These initial results are entirely in keeping with our larger theoretical expectations about the causal influence of mass opinion on welfare states. However, by themselves, they are insufficient to provide evidence of a causal relationship. Opinion surveys are at best descriptive regarding country-level processes, since the latter are not directly measured.[4]

What further evidence must we have to infer that welfare state differences are shaped by mass policy preferences? We need to take into account potentially confounding factors such as age composition and political institutions. This means that our estimates measure the influence of mass policy preferences rather than effects of *other* factors on welfare states.

The importance of multivariate controls can be appreciated in the context of Alesina and Glaesar's (2004, chap. 7) consideration of linkage between mass opinion and social policy outputs. Alesina and Glaesar present results of a simple statistical model linking overall welfare spending effort with economic development and a measure—drawn from the *World Values Surveys*—of the belief that income is influenced by luck. Alesina and Glaesar (2004:187) find evidence for a large and statistically significant policy effect of their mass opinion measure. But they proceed to argue that this relationship ultimately reflects the influence of political institutions and racial heterogeneity, *not* a genuine opinion/policy linkage (even though their statistical model contains *no* controls for these factors. This line of reasoning suggests, then, the merits of including controls of this sort when seeking to analyze the influence of mass policy preferences over welfare states.[5]

Other Independent Variables

Guided by past research, our analyses include controls for established sources of welfare state policy output (e.g., Flora and Alber 1981; Huber et al. 1993; Wilensky 2002; see also Quadagno 1994). Returning to table 2.2, per capita GDP, women's labor force participation, and the rate of immigration are important controls. Following the approach of Huber and Stephens (2000), women's labor force participation is coded with a one-year lag.

Political institutions are viewed by many scholars as exerting a significant influence over policy output (Weir, Orloff, and Skocpol 1988b; Immergut 1992; Swank 2002), especially the degree to which their constitutional design creates opportunities for social policy reforms to be blocked by organized interest groups. We follow Huber and Stephens (2001, chap. 3) by using a measure of the quantity of "veto points" within a polity. This item is a scale ($\alpha = .65$) of five separate dimensions of institutional arrangements: federalism, parliamentary vs. presidential system, the strength of bicameralism, the use of judicial review, and the use of proportional representation versus plurality rules. Higher scores indicate the existence of more veto points.[6]

Partisan control over the national legislature is a causal factor identified by the power resources tradition (e.g., Korpi 1989; Esping-Andersen 1990; Huber et al. 1993). The policy influence of left parties in government is viewed as facilitating the development of comprehensive benefits and service programs, and a measure of control of government by left parties captures this effect. Because of the particular importance of left party governance within the power resources tradition, we also consider a second measure capturing the cumulative years of left party control (Huber and Stephens 2001). Christian-democratic control of government represents a distinct source of partisan influence on welfare policymaking (Castles 1994; Misra and Hicks 1994), insofar as religious parties within Western Europe generally mix high levels of benefits with lower levels of public service delivery. The policymaking activities of secular conservative parties represents a third pole. These parties have tended to couple fiscal conservatism with greater priority given to private forms of social provision (Hicks 1999; Huber and Stephens 2001).[7]

Partisan control of government is itself shaped by policy preferences, insofar as preferences affect the behavior of voters and, in turn, the outcome of elections. To address this relationship, we estimate regression models by first excluding and then including the measures of partisan control over national legislatures. This allows us to infer whether and to what extent the effects of mass policy preferences on welfare states are mediated by their relationship to partisan control of government.[8]

Cross-Sectional Time-Series Analysis

The data in this chapter, and much of data analyzed in this book, are cross-sectional time-series data in which the unit of analysis is the country-year. This means that rather than the individual respondents whose attributes are probed in polls and surveys, it is *aggregate* opinion and country-level processes that are being measured. When we observe some (or all) countries over time, the data constitute a time series; hence the term *cross-sectional time-series data.*

Cross-sectional time-series data can provide powerful insights into the operation of country-level processes, but there are significant challenges as well. Data of this sort may be characterized by the presence of correlated errors, as when events in one country affect developments within others. This can violate classical assumptions regarding the independence of errors across observations (Greene 2000), and errors also tend to be heteroskedastic, possessing a nonconstant variance across observations. These conditions pose a challenge to statistical inference, for they can lead to biased estimates and misleading significance tests.

To correct for this possibility, we use a robust-cluster OLS approach to address correlated and non-identically distributed errors in the analysis. This approach has several advantages over earlier modeling strategies employed in the quantitative analysis of welfare states. One such approach, the Parks method, involves estimation of country-specific error correlation parameters. But as demonstrated by Beck and Katz (1995), under the conditions most frequently applying to country-level datasets this approach tends to underestimate standard errors by between 50 percent and 200 percent (resulting in overly optimistic significance tests). Prais-Winsten regression with a correction for serial correlation represents a second approach, but estimation of the serial correlation parameter requires data that are evenly spaced with respect to time intervals, and our OECD/ISSP data, like many other recent welfare state datasets, are characterized by countries contributing different numbers of observations spaced over unequal temporal intervals.

The robust-cluster approach is useful under these conditions. Like the more standard Huber-White estimator for heteroskedastic errors (see Long and Ervin 2000), the robust-cluster approach provides correct standard errors in the presence of unequal variance among the error terms. But unlike the Huber-White estimator, the robust-cluster approach remains valid in the presence of errors that are correlated within units, including serially correlated errors (Rogers 1993).[9]

In this context, two other approaches worthy of note are random-effects and fixed-effects models (Hsiao 1996). The fixed-effects approach is common in the analysis of individual-level (panel) data, where it provides one means of addressing omitted variable bias and other non-random error structures (where the latter are assumed time-invariant). But in analyzing cross-sectional time-series data, the limitations of the fixed-effects approach are generally quite severe. This is because fixed-effects yields a purely *within-country* analysis and estimation, even though many country-level datasets are characterized by greater *between-country* variance in comparison to time-series variance (Plumper, Troeger, and Manow 2005).[10]

A random-effects model represents an alternative approach to these econometric challenges, where information from the between- and within-estimators is pooled under the assumption that some sources of error are time-invariant and others are time-varying. By virtue of the complexity of these assumptions, the random-effects model is used less frequently than fixed-effects and OLS-based approaches. In the course of the analysis, we compare both random-effects and fixed-effects approaches to our robust-cluster model of the ISSP/OECD data, using Raftery's Bayesian Information Criterion (1995; see also Beck and Katz 2001). Results of these comparisons are informative, buttressing our use of the robust-cluster OLS approach.

Causal Inference and Endogeneity

An important concern for any model of country-level data is *endogeneity,* whereby one or more right-hand-side variables are correlated with an unobserved error term. Endogeneity can have several potential sources (e.g., Wooldridge 2002, chap. 4): the omission of a relevant variable; measurement error; or reverse causation/simultaneity bias, in which an explanatory variable is determined in part by the dependent variable. This is a potentially critical problem, for endogeneity would undermine confidence in any attempt at causal inference.

In this case, we are most concerned with the possibility that public preferences are influenced by the current operation of welfare state policies; that is, public support for social programs is a direct result of the programs themselves, not vice versa. If so, public opinion could not be said to exert any independent causal impact. Assertions about the existence of contemporaneous policy feedback of this sort have frequently been used to argue, a priori, against the influence of mass opinion over policy (e.g., Steinmo 1994; Immergut 1998). We must take such allegations seriously. But it is also important to emphasize that no systematic efforts have as yet been made to generate evidence for or against such assumptions.

Given concerns about reverse causation and other endogeneity scenarios, it is necessary to rule them out or, failing that, to employ an alternative estimator, such as two-stage least squares, that is better suited to handling such problems. To this end, we apply a test for endogeneity originally developed by Hausman (1978, 1983) and extended by Davidson and MacKinnon (1993). This test enables us to gauge whether endogeneity necessitates the use of two-stage least squares estimation, or whether the analyses can be conducted using simpler and more efficient single-equation methods.

It is important to emphasize that endogeneity by its nature involves *contemporaneous* processes in which an unobserved error influences an independent variable. The contemporaneous characterization is critical to grasp, for mass policy preferences, alongside virtually any right-hand-side variable, are potentially subject to influence at the hands of welfare state development itself. Indeed, our own theoretical approach and all past welfare state theories are compatible with such processes. A paradigmatic examples would be Huber and Stephens's (2000) establishment of women's labor force participation as a proximate source of welfare output that itself is influenced by earlier levels of social provision. Scholarship on the interrelationship of welfare state institutions and economic development (e.g., Garrett 1998; Hall and Soskice 2001) provides another example. We emphasize that it is *contemporaneous* feedback that would represent an instance of endogeneity bias and would thus be potentially incompatible with mass policy preferences (and any right-hand-side variable) exerting influence over welfare state output.[11]

Interaction Effects Involving Policy Preferences

Finally, we need to consider the possibility of interaction effects across policy regimes. Here, the issue is whether mass policy preferences have similar or different effects across national and temporal contexts. A reasonable starting assumption is that mass policy preferences influence welfare states in similar ways, regardless of the context. But a variety of plausible arguments suggest grounds for entertaining alternative hypotheses. Regarding temporal context, for instance, Jacobs and Shapiro (2000; see also Monroe 1998) have argued that policy responsiveness has declined over time in the United States. This implies one type of interaction: between policy preferences and time. A second scenario is that mass policy preferences operate differently across national borders. These would include the possibility of regime-based differences (e.g., Korpi and Palme 1998), higher levels of representation of citizen preferences within centralized polities or those employing proportional representation rules (e.g., Lijphart 1999; Powell 2000), or even a pattern of U.S. exceptionalism (e.g., Lipset 1996). We consider whether any of these possible interactions are significant and should be incorporated in subsequent models.

The chapter appendix provides the details of our tests relating to modeling strategy, endogeneity, and interactions. The results of those tests show that (1) the robust-cluster approach provides the best way of analyzing the data, (2) there is no evidence for endogeneity bias, and (3) there is no evidence of interactions involving policy preferences.

Effects of Policy Preferences on Welfare States

Table 2.3 displays coefficients and standard errors for three statistical models predicting welfare state effort in developed democracies. The differences between these models capture important theoretical propositions. Model 1 shows the effects of all variables except for partisan control over government. Model 2 then adds coefficients for the partisan control variables. By comparing coefficients across model 1 versus model 2, we can observe whether the total effects of mass policy preferences on welfare state effort are mediated by factors relating to partisan control over government. Model 2 allows us to evaluate the further possibility that the *cumulative* pattern of left party control (Huber and Stephens 2001) may itself be associated with mass policy preferences.

In model 1, results for established causal factors track those of previous studies. Economic development level and immigration level have negative effects on welfare state effort, though neither coefficient is significant in model 1. Women's labor force participation has a significant effect on spending effort, and the magnitude of this effect is large in both models. Coefficients for institutional veto points are not significant in either model.

Our primary interest is, of course, in the effects of mass policy preferences. Coefficients for policy preferences are significant in both models. These reveal a strong relationship between the policy preferences of national publics and welfare spending effort. The magnitude of these effects is substantial, even when compared to the effects of factors established in previous scholarship. In model 2, for example, a standard unit increase in mass preferences raises by 2.59 percentage points the level of welfare effort, while a standard unit increase in the level of left cabinet control raises it by just over 2 percentage points.

Comparing the coefficients for mass policy preferences in models 1 and 2 allows us to investigate the extent to which the influence of mass opinion is mediated by elections and partisan control over government. The 2.59

TABLE 2.3   **Coefficients and Robust-Cluster Standard Errors for Models of Welfare State Effort**

Independent Variables	Model 1		Model 2		Model 3	
Constant	12.30*	(4.59)	9.42*	(2.56)	18.13*	(6.41)
Year	<.01	(.15)	.27*	(.12)	.21	(.12)
Per capita GDP	−.30	(.19)	−.40*	(.10)	−.36*	(.13)
Immigration	−.43	(.36)	−.37	(.24)	−.46	(.13)
Women's labor force participation	.29*	(.13)	.28*	(.05)	.13	(.13)
Political institutions	1.90*	(.77)	.86	(.63)	2.09	(1.13)
Religious party control	—		.10*	(.01)	.05*	(.02)
Left party control	—		.05*	(.02)	—	
Cumulative left party control	—		—		.18	(.10)
Policy preferences	5.03*	(.78)	2.59*	(.69)	2.89*	(.94)
R^2	.61		.81		.74	

Note: Coefficients (unstandardized) estimated by OLS with robust-cluster standard errors; an asterisk next to a coefficient denotes significance at the .05 level.

coefficient in model 2 is substantial, and it retains just over half its magnitude from model 1. This result shows that while partisan composition of government mediates a good portion of the effects of mass policy preferences, mass preferences have an independent impact. This result provides powerful evidence for our larger theoretical argument concerning direct social policy responsiveness.

By comparing models 2 and 3, we can evaluate whether replacing the contemporaneous effect of partisan control over government with a cumulative measure of left party control changes our portrait of the influence of mass policy preferences. If the effects of policy preferences and cumulative left control are closely related, we expect the policy preference coefficients to decline in magnitude in model 3. But the main effects of policy preferences are actually slightly larger in model 3, suggesting little such overlap.[12]

In the remainder of this chapter's analyses, so as to err on the side of not overestimating the impact of public opinion, we employ the slightly more conservative estimates of policy preferences in model 2.

What Lies Behind Differences in Welfare State Effort?

The results of the previous section provide clear evidence that policy preferences exert a substantial influence over welfare state effort, and this operates both directly and indirectly (through elections). Turning to the next set of results, we decompose the contribution of independent variables to explaining cross-national differences in welfare state effort.[13] This allows us to gauge whether cross-national differences in preferences can explain key points of patterned variability in welfare state effort.

Starting with our analysis of regime-based differences, the decomposition estimates in table 2.4 enable us to gauge how much specific factors matter in accounting for differences in welfare state effort between social, Christian, and liberal democracies. Column entries in table 2.4 are the predicted percentage of the overall difference between social and liberal democratic welfare states (and between Christian and liberal welfare states) attributable to a row-specific factor using the coefficients from model 2. As an example, the estimate for women's labor force participation in the first column of the table indicates that 36 percent of the overall difference between social and liberal regimes is explained by higher levels of female labor force participation in social democracies.[14]

Regarding other established factors, partisan control over government (46 percent) is likewise central to policy differences between social and liberal democracies.

In table 2.4, the decomposition results show that just over a third (36 percent) of the difference in welfare state effort in social versus liberal democracies is accounted for by mass policy preferences. The next set of results is for factors behind the differences in welfare state effort in Christian versus liberal democracies, and these decompositions differ in two notable ways. First, both partisan control over government and mass policy preferences play a more extensive role in generating differences between Christian and liberal welfare states, accounting, respectively, for 67 and 63 percent of the spending differences. Second, by virtue of their negative signs, decomposition estimates for women's labor force participation anticipate *higher* levels of welfare state effort within liberal democracies.

How do these results advance our understanding of sources of differences in the size of welfare states across ideal-typical regimes? In line with the established wisdom, such forces as partisan politics and women's labor force participation are central to regime differences. More thematically, we can better see how mass policy preferences also matter, accounting for a

TABLE 2.4 **Decomposition of Between-Regime Differences in Overall Welfare State Effort within Social, Christian, and Liberal Democracies, 1997**

Independent Variables	Social vs. Liberal Democracies: [Model 2]	Christian vs. Liberal Democracies: [Model 2]
Economic and demographic factors		
Per capita GDP	−16%	22%
Immigration	8%	11%
Women's labor force participation	36%	−57%
Political institutions		
Veto points	−9%	−5%
Partisan control		
Control of government	46%	67%
Policy preferences		
Preferences	35%	63%
Σ Estimates[a]	100%	101%
OBSERVED DIFFERENCE IN WELFARE STATE EFFORT	*+11%*	*+8%*

[a]Decomposition estimates do not all sum to 100 percent due to rounding error.

sizable portion of between-regime differences in welfare spending output. Put another way, in comparison to liberal democracies, social and Christian democracies have higher levels of spending effort in part because these countries are characterized by greater citizen preference for public social provision.

To this point, the decompositions we have presented are for differences between clusters of countries representing different types of welfare states. How do they look when we consider specific pairs of countries? Given the ideal-typical nature of regimes, we can anticipate some differences with respect to between-country versus between-regime comparisons.

Starting with the decomposition of Swedish versus U.S. welfare state differences in table 2.5, we find that partisan control and mass policy preferences each account for 35 percent of overall spending differences. The next largest impact is represented by the 22 percent estimate for per capita GDP. In the second decomposition for Norway versus Canada, economic factors have far less relevance; it is partisan control (59%) and mass policy preferences (69%) that are the key sources of spending differences in these two welfare states.

In the table 2.6 decomposition of Germany versus Australia, partisan

TABLE 2.5 **Decomposition of Between-Country Differences in Overall Welfare State Effort for Specific Social and Liberal Democracies, 1997**

Independent Variables	Sweden vs. the United States [Model 2]	Norway vs. Canada [Model 2]
Economic and demographic factors		
Per capita GDP	22%	–44%
Immigration	11%	9%
Women's labor force participation	14%	19%
Political institutions		
Veto points	–16%	–13%
Partisan control		
Control of government	35%	59%
Policy preferences		
Preferences	35%	69%
Σ Estimates[a]	101%	99%
OBSERVED DIFFERENCE IN WELFARE STATE EFFORT	*+16%*	*+6%*

[a]Decomposition estimates do not all sum to 100 percent due to rounding error.

control over government is far and away the most important source of welfare state differences (63%). The next largest factor is mass policy preferences (28%). In the cases of Italy and Ireland, partisan politics is even more central (108%), with the decomposition estimates exceeding 100 percent because other factors (especially women's labor force participation) anticipate higher welfare state spending in Ireland. Policy preferences have, by contrast, a positive bearing, but a relatively small one (9%).

The Comparative Impact of Mass Policy Preferences

The novelty of policy preferences' influence over welfare states benefits by further perspective. Here, we wish to compare the magnitude of this influence with the impact of more established factors. To this end, we compare the respective effects of mass policy preferences with women's labor force participation and religious party control. Together, these factors represent the three largest sources of influence over welfare spending effort in our statistical models.

We present in figure 2.3 the results of our comparisons. Calculations are expressed in standard units, making direct comparisons possible. The first panel of the figure shows that the effects of women's labor force participa-

TABLE 2.6 **Decomposition of Between-Country Differences in Overall Welfare State Effort for Specific Christian and Liberal Democracies, 1997**

Independent Variables	Germany vs. Australis [Model 2]	Italy vs. Ireland [Model 2]
Economic and demographic factors		
Per capita GDP	3%	−11%
Immigration	8%	24%
Women's labor force participation	−5%	−36%
Political institutions		
Veto points	3%	6%
Partisan control		
Control of government	63%	108%
Policy preferences		
Preferences	28%	9%
Σ Estimates[a]	100%	100%
OBSERVED DIFFERENCE IN WELFARE STATE EFFORT	*+10%*	*+7%*

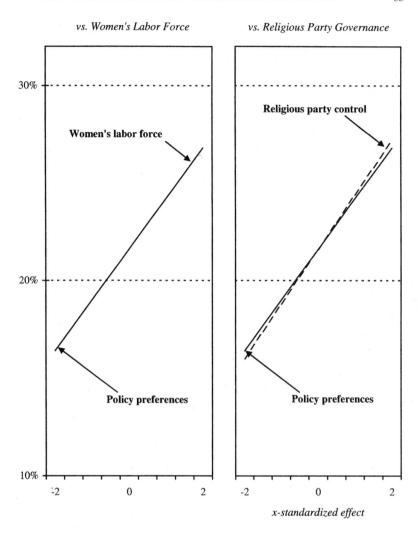

FIGURE 2.3. Predicted effects of policy preferences and two established factors on welfare state effort. Scores indicate levels of preference for welfare state provision, women's labor force participation, or degree of religious party control.

tion and policy preferences are indistinguishable in magnitude from one another. In the second panel, the further effects of religious party control are just slightly larger than those of mass policy preferences (and women's labor force participation). The key message of these calculations is that the policy influence of mass preferences compares favorably to established sources of welfare state policy output.

We can explore this issue further by predicting how welfare states in liberal democracies versus elsewhere might respond to new patterns of policy preference. For instance, how would the U.S. welfare state be different if Americans developed the same policy preferences as Norwegians, holding other differences between the countries constant? And how would the Norwegian welfare state fare with Americans' preferences regarding public social provision? We answer these and related questions with the calculations presented in figure 2.4, using 1997 as the time period for these calculations.

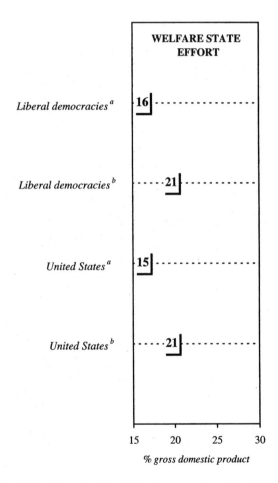

FIGURE 2.4. Predicted welfare state effort in liberal democracies and the United States, 1997: a. predicted values; b. predicted values with social-democratic level of policy preferences.

Starting with the figure 2.4 results for liberal democracies, 16 percent is the predicted level of welfare state effort within liberal democracies in 1997 using regime-specific covariate means. This 16 percent estimate provides us with a baseline for subsequent comparisons. The next estimate of 21 percent is the predicted level of welfare state effort we obtain by substituting the Norwegian level of policy preferences, holding constant all other variables. This substitution adds five percentage points, suggesting that Norwegian policy preferences, by themselves, would have pressured the liberal democratic welfare state to more closely resemble its Scandinavian counterpart.

The bottom half of figure 2.4 presents the same calculations for the United States. Substituting the social democratic mean has a very sizable impact on American welfare state effort. Specifically, by adding six percentage points of welfare spending effort, this would narrow considerably the gap between the social democratic regime and the market-oriented U.S. welfare state.

It is also important to understand the reciprocal power of policy preferences to alter welfare state policy activity within social and Christian democracies. Using the baseline prediction of 27 percent for social democracies in figure 2.5, substitution of the liberal democratic level of policy preferences results in a sizable four-percentage-point reduction in 1997 welfare effort. Estimates for Christian democracies present a similar portrait, for the baseline prediction of 24 percent welfare state effort drops by four percentage points under the assumption of a trend toward the level of policy preferences found within liberal democracies. In both Christian and social democracies, movement toward liberal-democratic levels of mass policy preferences would likely have been of real consequence in the 1990s.

Together, these results have powerful and strategic implications. Future efforts to alter policy preferences among citizens could, if successful, readily induce a shift in overall welfare output within democracies. Indeed, the adoption of a wholly different national or regional outlook could contribute to a shift in the overall direction of social policy. As we will see in chapter 5, the probability of this sort of shift actually occurring is not particularly high. Aggregate policy attitudes tend to change fairly slowly over time. But the present chapter's results indicate that strategic efforts to move policy preferences, when successful, could begin to alter the overall size and shape of the world's developed welfare states.

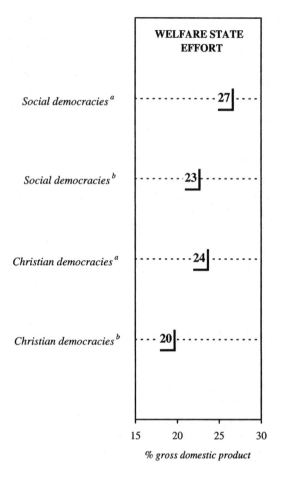

FIGURE 2.5. Predicted welfare state effort in social and Christian democracies, 1997: a. predicted values; b. predicted values with liberal-democratic level of policy preferences.

Conclusion

We have presented in this chapter the first critical test of our embedded preferences theory. We asked whether mass policy preferences can help account for some of the remarkable variability in the overall policy output of contemporary welfare states. The results we have developed in this chapter compel us to answer in the affirmative. We find that the policy preferences of national populations strongly influence aggregated welfare state spending. For instance, a standard unit increase in preferences for welfare state provision is predicted to raise the level of overall welfare state effort by over 2.5 percentage points. This compares favorably to more established effects of left party governance. But the social policy influence of preferences is slightly below the additional effect of religious party control, attesting to the multicausal nature of welfare policymaking.

Our results also demonstrate that mass opinion is consistently among the largest sources of cross-national patterning in the overall output of welfare states. Our decompositions reveal that policy preferences account for 35 percent of the differences between social and liberal democracies, and over 60 percent of spending differences between Christian and liberal democracies. Notably, the analyses also show that a substantial portion of the influence of policy preferences is direct, occurring independent of the partisan composition of national government.

The results of this chapter help to resolve the seeming paradox of large regime-based differences that has vexed contemporary welfare state scholarship. We have found that much of the influence of policy preferences on welfare states is direct, occurring independent of the partisan composition of national governments. This evidence for direct policy responsiveness is very much in keeping with the findings of U.S. research (e.g., Stimson et al. 1995; Wlezien 1995; Erikson et al. 2002a), where scholars have also unearthed pathways of direct influence. By considering these findings in comparative perspective, however, we are able to expand beyond the U.S.-centered debate. Claims about uniquely high levels of American responsiveness are put in proper perspective by the results we have developed.

In bringing opinion/policy research to the study of welfare states, our results also highlight the political significance of the growth of information about mass opinion in democracies (Geer 1996). In principle, such information is increasingly available to policymakers and even to ordinary citizens. For instance, it is virtually unthinkable within Scandinavia for political officials to be ignorant of the postwar development of comprehensive public provisions and the generally high levels of public support they have enjoyed (e.g., Svallfors 1997; Andersen et al. 1999; Arter 1999). Furthermore, the electoral dominance of left coalitions within Scandinavia has sent strong signals to *other* parties regarding public expectations concerning the welfare state. This illustrates, then, the ways in which competition between political parties and information concerning policy preferences undergird the operation of direct linkages between mass opinion and policy output. When crafting welfare state policies, government officials respond to citizens' preferences. That this is true of developed democracies as a whole attests to the robustness of conduits linking information about mass preferences to elected officials.

The central message of this chapter is that in order to understand cross-national differences in welfare states, including regime-based differences, we must understand the role of mass policy preferences in shaping social policy, and the tendency of government officials to respond to those preferences. Clearly, welfare states possess distinctive ideological foundations. The "three worlds" of welfare capitalism, in Esping-Andersen's (1990) famous characterization, are distinguished not only by economic, demographic, and partisan political dimensions, but also by forms of mass policy preferences that provide legitimacy to specific types of public (or private) social provision.

METHODOLOGICAL APPENDIX

Robust-Cluster versus Alternative Estimators

An initial step in our analysis is to establish a statistical approach that satisfactorily addresses errors in country-level data. As we noted earlier in the chapter, it is possible that a random- or fixed-effects model (Hsiao 1986) provides a potentially viable alternative to the robust-cluster approach. To test this possibility, we compare robust-cluster OLS with random- and fixed-effects models of welfare state spending effort. To gauge which approach is preferable, we use Raftery's (1995) Bayesian Information Criterion (BIC) to evaluate the fit of the three statistical models to our OECD/ISSP data. Negative BIC scores indicate a potentially acceptable fit, and the relevant decision-rule is to choose the model with the lowest score. As discussed by Raftery (1995:139), BIC differences of 0–2 and 2–6 suggest, respectively, weak and positive evidence; BIC differences of 6–10 and more than 10 suggest, respectively, strong and very strong evidence.

BIC for the fixed-effects model is 88, and the positively signed score indicates that the fixed-effects approach provides an unacceptable description of the data. The BIC score for the random-effects model is –24, suggesting a considerable improvement. However, at –43, the BIC score for the robust-cluster model provides unambiguous evidence that the robust-cluster approach is superior to *both* random- and fixed-effects. The robust-cluster approach thus provides the best way of accounting for our data. The coefficients and standard errors that we present in this chapter are based accordingly on it.

Hausman Tests for Endogeneity

We apply Hausman's specification test for endogeneity (1978, 1983) as a means of gauging relevant evidence for endogeneity bias. The Hausman test has two stages (Davidson and MacKinnon 1993). First, an instrument for the covariate to be tested with respect to endogeneity is constructed by regressing that variable on the other right-hand-side variables, saving the predicted values. In the second stage, coefficients for the instrumented covariate and all remaining variables (dropping one for purposes of identification) are estimated, with a significant coefficient for the former returning evidence of endogeneity.

Table 2.7 displays results of the tests for endogeneity in mass policy preferences. A significant coefficient would indicate the presence of endogeneity, whereas a non-significant coefficient indicates no such evidence. As shown in the first row of the table, the coefficient estimate using robust-cluster estimation does not achieve statistical significance, even if we use a generous $p < .10$ threshold. A further application of the endogeneity test, summarized in the second row of table 2.7, uses instead the random-effects estimator, and it yields similar results and thus an identical conclusion.

These specification test results are informative, providing evidence against the operation of short-term processes of "feedback" from welfare state output to mass policy preferences, and, more generally, the presence of a correlation between our policy preferences measure and an unobserved error. Recall that the Hausman test is a test for *contemporaneous* feedback; longer-term processes of influence in which welfare state development influences policy preferences (or any factor behind current welfare state policymaking) are both probable and uncontroversial, for these do not represent endogeneity bias.

TABLE 2.7 **Endogeneity Tests for Policy Preferences**

Estimator	Coefficient (s.e.)	p-value	N	Decision
1. Robust-Cluster OLS	−1.40 (1.02)	.19	44	Fail to reject H_0
2. Random-Effects	−1.54 (1.91)	.42	44	Fail to reject H_0

Note: Coefficient is for effect of the residuals from the first-stage regression.

Interactions Involving Mass Policy Preferences

Finally, we consider the possibility of interaction effects involving mass policy preferences. We evaluate whether coefficients for interactions between policy preferences and various temporal and national contexts are significant. Starting with the possibility that the effects of policy preferences vary over time, the coefficient for the interaction of policy preferences and year is small and not close to significance ($\beta = -.11$; s.e. $= .11$), even at a low threshold of $p < .10$. This suggests that the social policy influence of mass preferences has varied little in magnitude during the contemporary historical era.

Considering next the interaction between policy preferences and the U.S. context, we find no evidence for this interaction ($\beta = 2.54$; s.e. $= 1.80$). The more general interaction between policy preferences and all liberal democracies is small and not significant ($\beta = -.14$; s.e. $= 3.18$). The coefficient for the interaction of policy preferences and Christian democracies ($ = -.30$; s.e. $= 2.85$) is not close to achieving significance; the same is true for the interaction between policy preferences and social democracies ($\beta = 2.39$; s.e. $= 4.16$). With respect to political institutions/veto points, we find no evidence for an interaction involving policy preferences ($\beta = 1.37$; s.e. $= .77$).

CHAPTER THREE

Retrenchment, Restructuring, Persistence

U ntil quite recently, welfare states in developed democracies were viewed by many commentators bitten by the globalization thesis as spiraling steadily into decline. Pointing to increasing flows of capital across national borders, labor unions' shrinking memberships, and the ascendancy of free trade ideologies since the end of the cold war, these commentators argued that high levels of public provision were becoming difficult to sustain (e.g., Brown 1988; Marklund 1988; Schwartz 1994). As one analyst put it, "Governments simply cannot pursue further economic regulation or increase spending on services as they did during the post-war boom" (Taylor-Gooby 1999:2).

The most common reason for anticipating welfare state decline relates to negative pressures exerted by economic globalization (Greve 1996; Standing 1999; Gilbert 2002). This was seen as a particularly severe problem for small European polities, whose economies depend upon the maintenance of close connections to global markets. The growing international mobility of capital is thought to weaken unions and left parties, while enhancing the attractiveness of market-oriented policies. Pressures to scale back welfare provisions and social expenditure in such an environment would seem inevitable. While critics have lamented the "race to the bottom" apparently ushered in by economic globalization (Rodrik 1997; Tonelson 2000), proponents welcome the prospect that global pressures may limit the regulatory and redistributive capacities of national governments (Ohmae 1996:141). What these normative evaluations share, however, is the assumption that recent patterns of globalization contribute to welfare state retrenchment.

Certainly, globalization theorists have pointed to real changes in the international environment, and to new pressures on the welfare state. But are contemporary welfare states truly in decline? Are recent patterns of change in the global economy ultimately incompatible with the welfare state? Will privatization and deregulated markets be the hallmark of twenty-first-century political economies?

These questions have received considerable attention in recent years, and a surprising and rather decisive conclusion has emerged: while there have been significant cuts to a number of specific social programs, the scenario of a universal decline in the welfare state has not occurred (Iversen 2001; Swank 2002; Castles 2004). The possible link between globalization and welfare state trends has also been investigated, and here too the results are clear. Using established measures of overall social policy output, economic globalization appears to have a very limited impact on welfare states (Iversen and Cusack 2000; Brady, Beckfield, and Seeleib-Kaiser 2005; Brooks and Manza 2006b). The negative effects of foreign direct investment, in particular, appear to have been exaggerated.

In retrospect, such results accord well with seminal earlier work on the capacity of national governments to respond strategically to the uncertainties posed by the global economy (Katzenstein 1985; Hall and Soskice 2001). This strain of institutionalist thinking received less attention at the time than popular claims about globalization in the 1980s and 1990s. But the inadequacies of economic globalization theory have led to a new appreciation for the robustness of the small West European polities (Katzenstein 2003). A subsequent insight is that social policy innovation in the form of jobs training programs and generous child-care provisions can have *positive* effects on citizens' productivity and labor-force attachments. Government provisions can enhance economic development and global competitiveness for countries such as Austria or Finland.[1]

Restructuring and Persistence

The new bottom line of comparative research is that wholesale retrenchment is a rare event. Welfare states are not as easily remade as neoliberal commentators once thought (cf. Samuelson 1997). It is striking that many European countries actually expanded the size of their welfare states during the 1980s and 1990s, developing new entitlement programs or increasing social spending outlays.

Yet amidst evidence of the absence of universal retrenchment are the

results of numerous studies documenting declines in specific social programs.[2] Indeed, it is within domains such as unemployment and sickness
benefits that cutbacks are most apparent, communicating a new willingness on the part of government officials to contain costs, establish work
requirements, or impose longer waiting periods on individuals' access to
cash benefits. These developments have signaled to many commentators
an end to the "golden era" of postwar welfare state growth. "Restructuring" and its cognates have become the description of choice to capture
policy developments since the 1990s (Kuhnle and Alestalo 2000; Pierson
2001a; Rothstein and Steinmo 2002).

There is tension between evidence, on the one hand, that overall welfare state retrenchment is a rare event but, on the other, that specific program cuts or revisions are nonetheless common. These apparent contradictions can be resolved once we acknowledge that cuts in one type of program may be offset by expansion in other social programs. Policy-specific
provisions relating, for instance, to pensions or unemployment benefits
are most informative when they are coupled with analysis of the *overall* policy output of welfare states. For instance, in Sweden (e.g., Lindbom 2001; Kautto et al. 2001a, b) and the United States (e.g., Weaver
2000; Hacker 2002), programmatic revisions to unemployment and means-
tested welfare benefits respectively represent important examples of cuts
that in both cases were partly offset by trends in other social policy domains.

Clearly, the contemporary era is one marked by a variety of developmental patterns. While the overall shape and size of the welfare state appears least susceptible to full-blown retrenchment pressures, cuts or programmatic change within specific social policy domains have been more
common. Analysis of trends that focuses solely on specific domains or
spending programs may thus provide misleading results when generalized
to the welfare state as a whole. Our approach is to couple analysis of trends
in overall spending with that of trends in domain-specific programs to fully
capture the dynamics of retrenchment, restructuring, and persistence.

However compatible high levels of social spending have been with economic globalization, political and economic pressures on the welfare state
have shifted since the postwar era of programmatic expansion. Many of
the forces that underlay welfare state expansion have eroded. Challenges
to specific programs and the legitimacy of the welfare state have grown.
Accounting for the specific mechanisms behind the persistence of high levels of welfare state effort thus represents a new and different agenda for

theory and research. And the possibility that the mechanisms of persistence differ from those generating the original pressures behind welfare state emergence is likely. The dynamics of twenty-first-century capitalism may involve "new risks" that inhibit the replacement of social policy by markets, alongside a "new politics" of persistence and change (Esping-Andersen 1996a; Pierson 2001a).

The Question, Again, of Mass Policy Preferences

Unpacking mechanisms behind the phenomenon of welfare state persistence is the task we set ourselves in this chapter. Our theoretical account of embedded preferences provides one set of propositions about persistence tendencies in the overall shape and scope of welfare states. Within developed democracies, mass policy preferences exert significant pressures on the direction of welfare state development, with high levels of welfare support lowering the likelihood of retrenchment.

Our theoretical expectations have affinity with path dependency theorizing, particularly when its key concept of the "new constituencies" of the welfare state is broadened to encompass mass policy preferences (cf. Pierson 1996, 2001a, 2001b). We expect that pro-welfare state interest groups will have their greatest impact when the signals they communicate are congruent with the preferences of ordinary citizens as a whole. Likewise, the rationality of elected officials' "credit-claiming" strategies makes best sense under the assumption that voters prefer in the aggregate the maintenance or expansion of social programs. It would be extremely costly for politicians to incorporate policies championed by interest groups if those recommendations diverge substantially from those endorsed by the electorate.

As in the case of cross-national variation, previous scholarship has thus leaned in notable ways toward mass opinion as a mechanism that may protect popular welfare states. But there have been no empirical efforts to estimate its impact on the maintenance of the welfare state. Our investigation in this chapter thus extends our larger consideration of the social policy influence of mass opinion. As before, we must take into account potentially confounding influences on welfare state development. We also complement our primary focus on aggregated welfare state output with additional, finer-grained examination of specific social policy domains.

Data and Measures

Analysis of the contributions of policy preferences to persistence tendencies in welfare states requires cross-national and over-time standardization of measures, a point we emphasized in chapter 2. To address these requirements, we again make use of our merged ISSP/OECD dataset containing observations for sixteen democracies covering select years in the 1980–2000 period. Because of the complexities of the overall versus domain-specific trends that underlie restructuring and persistence tendencies, we supplement our analysis of overall welfare spending effort with four additional measures of social policy outputs: welfare transfers; benefits generosity; sickness benefits; and per-capita public health spending. These measures are useful in capturing not only the complexity of domain-specific trends, but also the ways in which such trends can diverge substantially in comparison to patterns of change in the overall output of welfare states.

There are three main steps in the analyses we present in this chapter. First, we examine the pattern of recent trends in overall welfare state spending effort, considering change in specific countries as well as ideal-typical regimes. The trend analyses enable us to corroborate the scholarly consensus concerning welfare state persistence. They provide a point of departure for what follows.

In the second part of the analyses, we consider trends involving specific social policy domains, below the level of aggregated welfare output. We also probe the contrast between cash-centered measures and measures that span both cash transfers *and* services. These analyses substantiate the conclusion that it is the aggregated output of welfare states that most clearly displays persistence tendencies.

We present our explanatory analyses in the third section. For these analyses, we simulate the impact on welfare states of a variety of substantively meaningful temporal trends in independent variables. We focus on mass policy preferences (alongside women's labor-force participation and economic development) as key sources of persistence or change relating to developmental tendencies in welfare states.

Aggregate and Domain-Specific Measures of Welfare State Output

Our principal measure of welfare state policy focuses on the *aggregated* spending output of welfare states. It is the same as in chapter 2, derived

from the *Social Expenditures Database* (OECD 2005). As summarized in
table 3.1, our trend analysis of overall welfare effort supplements multivariate analysis of the merged ISSP/OECD dataset (N = 44) with nearly
complete observations for eighteen democracies during the period from
1980 through 2001 (N = 360). Because the *Social Expenditures Database*
begins in 1980, we also consider pre-1980 trends using the OECD's earlier
and more restricted measure of welfare state transfers.

Our third dependent variable, benefits generosity, is a more focused
measure. It summarizes cash entitlements across the three domains of pensions, unemployment benefits, and sickness benefits (Scruggs 2004). Like
the welfare state transfers measure, it ignores service provision, but unlike

TABLE 3.1   **Dependent Variables in the Analysis**

Variable	Description	Data Source
Overall welfare state effort[a]	Government expenditures on cash and in-kind benefits and services (9 categories)[b] as a percentage of GDP	OECD *Social Expenditures Database* (SOCX)
Welfare state transfers[c]	Social security transfers as a percentage of GDP.	OEDC *Historical Statistics,* various years
Benefits generosity[d]	Index of average income replacement for pensions, unemployment benefits, and sickness benefits.	*Welfare State Entitlements Dataset* (WSI)
Sickness benefits[e]	Ratio of net insurance benefit for general short-term illness paid to a singel person earning the APW wage.	WSI
Per capita public health spending[f]	Per capita public expenditures on health, purchasing power parity (PPP) adjusted to 2000 U.S. dollars.	SOCX

[a]Country-years in trend analysis: Australia (1980–2001), Austria (1990–2001), Belgium, Canada, Denmark, Finland, France, Germany, Ireland, Italy, Japan, Netherlands (1980–2001), New Zealand (1980–2001), Norway (1988–2001), Spain, Sweden, Switzerland, the United Kingdom, and the United States (1980–2001)
[b]Old-age benefits, survivor benefits, disability and sickness benefits, health services, family benefits and services, active labor market programs, unemployment benefits, housing, and residual provisions.
[c]Country-years in trend analysis: Australia, Austria, Belgium, Canada, Denmark, Finland, France, Germany, Ireland, Italy, Japan, Netherlands, New Zealand, Norway, Sweden, Switzerland, the United Kingdom, and the United States (1960–1980)
[d]Country-years in trend analysis: Australia, Austria, Belgium, Canada, Denmark, Finland, France, Germany, Ireland, Italy, Japan, Netherlands, New Zealand, Norway, Sweden, Switzerland, the United Kingdom, and the United States (1980–2001)
[e]Country-years in trend analysis: Australia (1980–2001), Austria (1980–2000), Belgium (1980–1999), Canada (1980–2001), Denmark (1983–2001), Finland, France, Germany, Ireland, Italy, Japan (1980–2001), Netherlands (1980–2000), New Zealand (1980–2001), Norway, Sweden, Switzerland (1983–2000), the United Kingdom, and the United States (1980–2001)
[f]Country-years in trend analysis: Australia (1980–2001), Austria (1990–2001), Belgium, Canada, Denmark, Finland, France, Germany, Ireland, Italy, Japan, Netherlands (1980–2001), New Zealand (1980–2001), Norway (1988–2001), Spain, Sweden, Switzerland, the United Kingdom, and the United States (1980–2001)

the transfers measure it does not include further entitlement domains such as family cash benefits (as well as means-tested benefits in such domains as housing). In line with recent arguments that generous welfare states have become more service-intensive *and* cash-entitlement-stingy (Huber and Stephens 2001), we expect the benefits generosity index to reveal greater evidence of negative welfare state trends.

Our final pair of dependent variables provide a further perspective on the specificity of developmental trends in overall versus domain-specific policy outputs. As summarized in table 3.1, the first of these is for the domain of sickness benefits, where these data measure the level of government-provided replacement income for conditions of short-term illness (Scruggs 2004). As discussed further in the results section, we focus on this replacement income measure because it informatively documents the *most* extensive pattern of welfare state retrenchment *and* because of the methodological argument advanced on behalf of replacement ratio indices (Allan and Scruggs 2004). The second domain-specific measure is for public health spending (OECD 2005), where these are purchasing power parity-adjusted (PPP-adjusted) data showing government spending per capita. Data for the two domains-specific measures are available in most countries for the entire 1980–2001 period.[3]

Independent Variables

Independent variables in our multivariate analyses are the same as those considered in chapter 2 (table 2.2). These variables measure established sources of welfare state development associated with logic of industrialism, political institutions, and power resources approaches. As before, mass policy preferences represent the novel factor in the analysis. Complementing the cross-sectional comparisons in chapter 2, our focus in this chapter is on the temporal dimension of welfare state variability, that is, the degree to which states have experienced change over time.

Results

Trends in Overall Welfare Effort

We consider first the nature of trends in overall welfare output within developed democracies. Using our primary measure of aggregated social spending effort, the data in figure 3.1 support scholarly consensus regard-

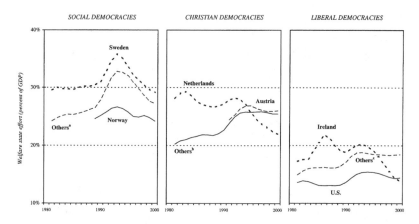

FIGURE 3.1. Country-specific trends in welfare state effort, 1980–2000 (3-year moving averages): a. Others = average for Denmark and Finland; b. Others = average for Belgium, France, Germany, Italy, Spain, and Switzerland; c. Others = average for Australia, Canada, Japan, New Zealand, and United Kingdom.

ing the absence of universal retrenchment trends. The figure's panels show three-year moving averages for trends in overall welfare effort within specific social democracies, Christian democracies, and liberal democracies. To facilitate interpretation, we present data for specific countries that experience distinctive patterns of change. Countries with more similar temporal patterns are summarized under estimates for "Others" to provide a further point of comparison.

Starting with the results for Sweden, welfare state spending during the 1980s was stable at 30 percent of gross domestic product, rising to approximately 36 percent by 1993, but moving back toward earlier levels by the late 1990s. Swedish welfare state spending during the past two decades thus shows a pattern of fluctuation but little evidence of a net decline, in keeping with conclusions of past studies (Stephens 1996; Lindbom 2001; Kautto et al. 2001a, b). In contrast, the shorter data series for Norway suggests considerably less variation about a lower level of effort (approximately 25 percent of GDP). The combined estimates for Denmark and Finland fall between those of Sweden and Norway, showing a cyclical pattern of late-1980s increases that were subsequently offset by cutbacks during the 1990s.

While the Scandinavian democracies had the highest overall level of welfare state spending during the 1980s, the continental Christian democracies experienced a dramatic increase during the following decade (Iversen 2001; Castles 2002; Swank 2002). This trend can be observed in the second panel of figure 3.1, where the data show that the expansion of the early 1990s was followed by a period of stability in Christian-democratic welfare states. The exception to this pattern is the Netherlands, whose 28–29 percent welfare state effort during the early 1980s was more characteristic of the social-democratic regime type. In the 1990s, however, the Dutch welfare state declined by a substantial five percentage points, revealing a significant retrenchment trend.

Turning to the third panel in figure 3.1, we see that most liberal democracies experienced a modest increase in welfare effort that was concentrated during the late 1980s and early 1990s. Since that time, spending effort has tended to be stable, including in the United States. The single exception is the case of Ireland, where a clear downward trend in welfare effort unfolded during the 1990s; Irish social spending did not keep up with the remarkable expansion of the economy during this time. In general, the liberal democracies continue to be characterized by comparatively low levels of spending effort throughout this period.

To provide another perspective on the 1980–2000 era, we present in figure 3.2 further trend analysis using the more restricted OECD measure of social security transfer spending for 1960 through 1980. The results of these analyses are easy to summarize: changes affecting most welfare states show—as expected—a pattern of expansion during those decades, with the rate of growth within a handful of countries slowing by the late 1970s. The two decades prior to 1980 were thus characterized by substantial increases in welfare state spending, especially within the social and Christian democracies of Western Europe, and (to a slightly lesser extent) among the liberal democratic regimes.

Using the OECD's transfers spending measure as a baseline, it is clear that the dramatic pattern of welfare state growth during the 1960s and 1970s has yet to be repeated, and declines in most social democracies during the 1990s caution strongly against assumptions about the inevitability of welfare state growth. By the same token, however, the inverted-U-shaped pattern of trends within Scandinavia still left spending effort within social democracies largely unchanged since 1980 (and much higher in the Finnish case). At an average of 26.2 percent of GDP, social-democratic spending effort remains the highest among regime types, and it thus appears misleading to characterize recent temporal patterns as indicative of retrenchment in the overall shape of welfare states. Overall, only two of the eighteen OECD countries we consider show a net decline (and thus

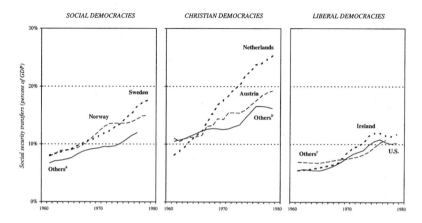

FIGURE 3.2. Country-specific trends in social security transfers, 1960–1980 (three-year moving averages): a. Others = average for Denmark and Finland.; b. Others = average for France, Germany, Italy, and Switzerland; c. Others = average for Australia, Canada, Japan, New Zealand, and United Kingdom.

retrenchment) in their levels of social spending effort during the past two decades. By contrast, thirteen of the eighteen countries have experienced an increase in welfare effort during this time, and the magnitude of this increase has been pronounced in several Christian democracies.

Restructuring and Domain-Specific Trends

We are now in position to extend our portrait of persistence tendencies in welfare states to consider other trends involving restructuring and retrenchment. These patterns can be observed by focusing on finer-grained measures of social policy outputs, and a useful place to start is with our third dependent variable, for average benefits generosity. By design, this measure is restricted to cash benefits, ignoring social services provision. If welfare state restructuring has involved a recalibration of cash entitlements, we expect the benefits generosity measure to return greater evidence for negative trends. This is precisely what we find in figure 3.3: a majority of welfare states are characterized by a decline in average benefits generosity during the 1990s. Looking over the entire period (1980 through 2000), seven of our eighteen countries experienced a net reduction in benefits generosity, showing the greater likelihood of retrenchment trends in policy domains involving cash entitlements.

The greatest rollback is for sickness benefits. Figure 3.4 reveals that half

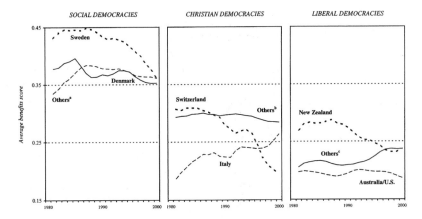

FIGURE 3.3. Country-specific trends in benefits generosity, 1980–2000 (three-year moving averages): a. Others = average for Finland and Norway; b. Others = average for Austria, Belgium, France, Germany, and Netherlands; c, Others = average for Canada, Ireland, Japan, and United Kingdom.

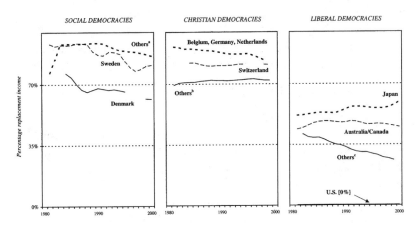

FIGURE 3.4. Country-specific trends in sickness benefits provision, 1980–2000 (3-year moving averages): a. Others = Norway and Finland; b. Others = Austria, France, and Italy; c. Others = Ireland, New Zealand, and United Kingdom.

of the countries under consideration experienced retrenchment, using the sickness benefits data in the *Welfare State Entitlements* dataset (Scruggs 2004). The net reduction in replacement income shows as much as a 52 percent decline in the United Kingdom, 26 percent in New Zealand, and 23 percent in Denmark.

Clearly, then, retrenchment trends within specific policy domains can be extensive. Yet it is important to again emphasize that evidence for retrenchment in sickness benefits is not tantamount to retrenchment in the overall output of welfare states. In this context, the *cash benefits* focus of replacement income measures suggests a second thematic point, namely, that many policy-specific domains of modern welfare states also involve a large service component. Indeed, in the domain of public health policy, a large majority of government health policy output is services-related: consultation and provision of doctor visits, hospitalization and surgical procedures, and prescription medication rather than cash (sickness) benefits.

This centrality of services to the key domain of health policy can be appreciated more directly by considering the percentage of public health spending that is devoted to cash benefits. In Figure 3.5, we present social expenditure data from the OECD (2002b) that documents this ratio, first for the United States and Sweden, and then for the other sixteen democracies in our analysis. On average, cash benefits constitute only 8 percent of all public health spending in democracies. In Sweden, this figure has risen as high as approximately 26 percent, and fallen as low as 12 percent, while the United States averages just 5 percent. In no country are the cash dimensions of health spending close to half of all spending, and the over-time trend is for the cash benefits percentage to decrease. The latter point underscores the *growing* importance of services to public health policy in the contemporary era.

Taken together, these considerations demonstrate how an exclusive focus on either services or cash benefits to the exclusion of the other provides a potentially misleading portrait of trends and cross-national differences in specific social policy domains. This can be seen using a further measure of the public health domain that is summarized in figure 3.6. Here, we use OECD expenditure data that summarize per capita government health spending, where this includes cash benefits *and* social services, and measurement is in 2000 U.S. dollars (adjusted to reflect cross-national and temporal differences in PPP).

In contrast to the picture conveyed by the sickness benefits data, the measure in figure 3.6 shows that per capita health spending has risen in all developed democracies, though the rates of increase vary considerably across countries and regime types. This does not mean that the two health-policy-specific measures are incompatible. Instead, it shows that a dual focus on cash benefits and services is appropriate when considering time

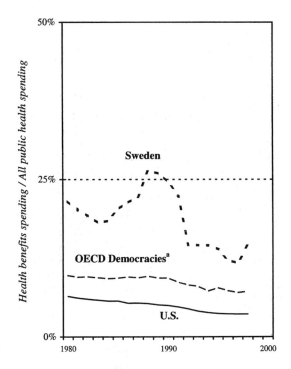

FIGURE 3.5. What percent of public health provision are cash benefits? a. Others = Australia, Austria, Belgium, Canada, Denmark, Finland, France, Germany, Ireland, Italy, Japan, Netherlands, New Zealand, Sweden, Switzerland, United Kingdom, and United States (short series for Norway not included).

trends and cross-national differences in many social policy domains. In doing so, this consideration of domain-specific measures again suggests the utility of an aggregated measure of overall welfare state output as providing inclusive summaries across the range of social policy domains.

Analyzing Welfare State Persistence

A small army of globalization theorists once argued that welfare states would experience substantial retrenchment. We find, as have previous scholars, that such claims are overblown when it comes to the aggregated output of welfare states. But what forces have exerted temporal pressures on the overall shape and output of contemporary welfare states? Do mass policy preferences, in particular, contribute to persistence tendencies?

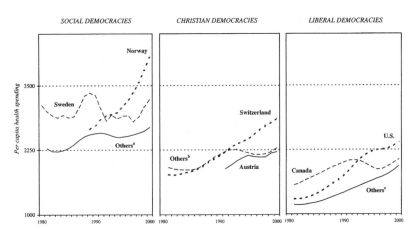

SOCIAL DEMOCRACIES   CHRISTIAN DEMOCRACIES   LIBERAL DEMOCRACIES

FIGURE 3.6. Country-specific trends in per capita public health spending, 1980–2000 (three-year moving averages): a. Others = average for Denmark and Finland; b. Others = average for Belgium, France, Germany, Italy, Netherlands, and Spain; c. Others = average for Australia, Ireland, Japan, New Zealand, and United Kingdom.

To answer these questions, our point of departure is the statistical model of welfare effort that we established in chapter 2. Recall that this model is estimated for the merged ISSP/OECD data, and the dependent variable is overall welfare state spending relative to gross domestic product. For these analyses, we use coefficients from our statistical model to predict welfare spending output under different, theoretically relevant conditions. These include trends in which all countries approach the level of policy preferences represented by the United States, and, in turn, by Norway (holding constant other covariates at their observed levels). This allows us to simulate the effect of specific *temporal* patterns of change on welfare state output. It is well known that mass support for welfare states in many countries shows considerable stability, or, in some cases, growing support (Smith 1987; Svallfors 1997; Andersen et al. 1999). For this reason, it is only through simulations that we can systematically gauge evidence for the contribution of these temporal patterns to welfare state persistence.[4]

We emphasize that mass policy preferences share with a number of other country-level variables a degree of temporal stability in their respective distributions. This distributional characteristic does not, however, disqualify these variables as causal factors behind social policymaking. For instance, political-institutional attributes exhibit *perfect* temporal stability over the time period we consider. But that does not disqualify this factor from operating as an input to social policymaking. Rather than explaining *change,* then, relatively stable temporal patterns in the level of mass policy preferences are expected to exert pressures toward stability and thus *persistence* in welfare states.[5]

Turning to our analysis of sources of welfare state persistence, we focus on three sets of countries (Norway, Germany/Italy, and Australia/United States) during the time period from 1991 to 1997. These countries exemplify the social-democratic, Christian-democratic, and liberal welfare state types, and we have full information in the ISSP/OECD dataset for all five countries in 1991 and 1997. Thus, we can use the relevant country-/time-specific covariate levels with the information contained in the coefficients to develop our simulation estimates.[6]

Figure 3.7 summarizes the results for Norway, with the first panel showing *baseline* estimates for the predicted level of welfare state effort from 1991 to 1997. These estimates are obtained by using *no* manipulation in covariate levels. They reveal temporal stability in Norwegian welfare effort during the 1990s.[7]

This figure's second panel investigates two further scenarios. In scenario 2, we simulate the effect of a movement toward 1997 levels of women's labor force participation in Norway. In scenario 3, we simulate the effect of

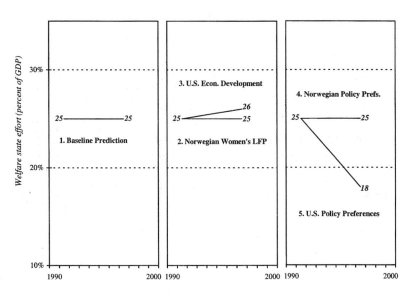

FIGURE 3.7. Predicted trends in welfare state effort, Norway

a movement toward 1997 levels of U.S. economic development. Scenario 2 has no effect on the current estimates, because we are considering the case of Norway. However, the movement in scenario 3 to the U.S. level of economic development predicts a one-percentage-point net *increase* in Norwegian welfare effort. This result is due to slightly higher levels of per capita GDP in Norway during the 1990s.

The results for scenarios 4 and 5 are presented in the last panel of figure 3.7. Because scenario 4 simulates the 1997 level of Norwegian policy preferences, it is identical to the baseline prediction. But scenario 5 simulates U.S. levels of policy preferences instead. It produces a dramatic result: an additional *seven*-percentage-point decline in Norwegian welfare state effort during the 1990s. This means that if Norwegians developed the same policy preferences as Americans, retrenchment would have likely ensued. Such a result underscores the importance of (high) levels of policy preferences to persistence tendencies in the Norwegian welfare state.

In figure 3.8 we present parallel results for Christian-democratic Germany. In keeping with the observed trend data, the baseline prediction for Germany is a six-percentage-point increase in welfare effort between 1991 and 1997. In scenario 2, a movement to higher levels of women's labor force participation increases German welfare state effort by an *additional*

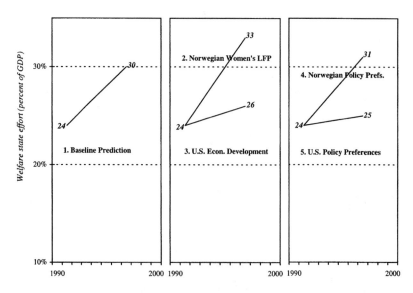

FIGURE 3.8. Predicted trends in welfare state effort, Germany

three percentage points. The scenario 3 simulation of a trend toward U.S. economic development levels reduces the baseline trend by four percentage points.

The third panel in the figure presents our simulations based on changes in the German level of mass policy preferences. In scenario 4, a movement toward the Norwegian level of policy preferences adds another percentage point to the trend in German welfare state effort during the 1990s. In scenario 5, a trend toward the U.S. level of policy preferences reduces German welfare state effort by five percentage points. A movement toward the much lower level of welfare state support exemplified by the United States had the potential to substantially rein in trends in Germany.

What of the case of the United States itself? Our results are summarized in figure 3.9, and few of the simulation scenarios significantly alter the baseline trajectory of the American welfare state in the 1990s. For scenarios 3 and 5, this is to be expected, since these simulations use the U.S. level of covariates. But in scenario 2, a trend toward the Norwegian level of women's labor-force participation adds only one percentage point to 1997 U.S. welfare effort; this is because American women's labor force participation is already quite high, resembling that of Norway's.

The scenario that shows the greatest temporal impact within the United

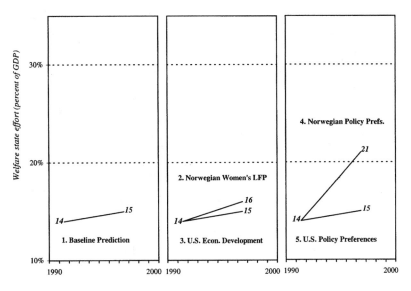

FIGURE 3.9. Predicted trends in welfare state effort, United States

States involves a trend toward the Norwegian level of policy preferences. Scenario 4, in which American attitudes are set to those of Norwegians, yields a six-percentage-point net increase in American welfare state development during the 1990s. This result is striking. It suggests the relevance of temporal patterns of U.S. policy preferences to understanding the (stable) trajectory of the American welfare state during the 1990s.

How do these country-specific results change when we consider clusters of countries making up a specific type of welfare regime? We address this question through simulations for Christian democracies (Germany and Italy) and liberal democracies (Australia and the United States), noting that the only social democracy available for analysis of the 1991–1997 time period is Norway. Results for Christian democracies are presented in figure 3.10.

In general, the Christian-democratic results are comparable to the earlier results for Germany. Trends toward the Norwegian levels of women's labor-force participation add considerably to welfare state expansion in the 1990s. In contrast, the substitution of Norwegian policy preferences has a much more modest effect. But simulation of the U.S. level of policy preferences generates a massive trend toward declining welfare effort. For its part, simulation of the U.S. level of economic development yields a

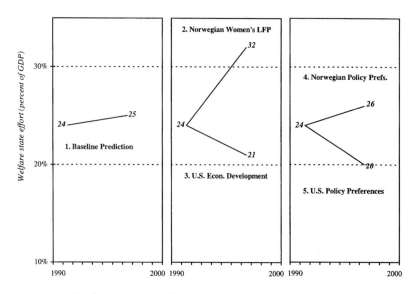

FIGURE 3.10. Predicted trends in welfare state effort, Christian democracies

four-percentage-point net reduction in welfare effort by 1997, an estimate identical to the one obtained earlier for Germany.

Results for the liberal democracies of Australia and the United States are presented in figure 3.11. The trend in scenario 2 toward Norwegian levels of women's labor force participation adds two percentage points to the baseline prediction, and the scenario 3 trend toward U.S. economic development levels reduces the baseline prediction by two percentage points. In scenario 4, simulating Norwegian policy preferences adds five percentage points, while the scenario 5 simulation of U.S. policy preferences reduces by one percentage point the baseline trend. Echoing the earlier U.S.-centered simulations, these results provide evidence for the relevance of temporal patterns of mass policy preferences to the recent trajectory of liberal welfare states.

Taken in summary, then, our simulations of a variety of negative as well as positive pressures enable us to better gauge the relative importance of key factors behind recent welfare state trajectories. Clearly, economic and demographic factors are important. Our simulations also show the relevance of current levels of mass policy preferences, where these contribute notably to welfare state persistence within social and Christian democracies.

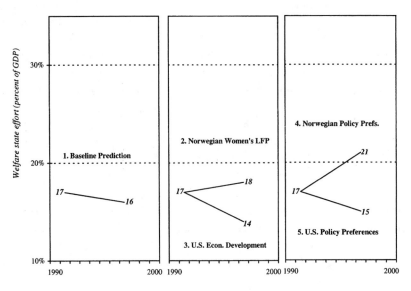

FIGURE 3.11. Predicted trends in welfare state effort, liberal democracies.

Conclusion

The possibility that welfare states in the age of globalization were beginning to experience a substantial decline animated a wide-ranging set of debates that have only recently begun to reach closure. Central to their res-
olution is the growing consensus among scholars that retrenchment in the
overall size and shape of welfare states is a rare event. The OECD's *Social
Expenditures Database* (2005) confirms this emerging scholarly consensus.
Only two of the eighteen countries we have investigated are characterized
by a net decline in social spending effort, while thirteen experienced an *increase* in welfare effort between 1980 and 2001, and the remaining three
show little net change.

Furthermore, economic globalization, the main culprit behind predictions of welfare state demise, now appears to have been vastly overstated
as a potential source of policy redirection. One key mechanism of globalization, foreign direct investment, has at best an inconsistent (and modest)
relationship to welfare state output (Brady et al. 2005). Related historical
processes such as deindustrialization may even contribute to welfare state
growth (Iversen 2001).

We have argued for the importance of aggregated welfare state expenditure as essential to systematic consideration of developmental trends.
But we also examined domain-specific measures that highlight important
trends in cash benefits provision. We showed how domain-specific trends
can provide a misleading portrait of the trajectory of *overall* welfare state
development. This does not mean that retrenchment cannot occur within
specific policy domains, for it clearly has in domains such as sickness benefits within many countries. But alongside such developments are important expansions within *other* policy domains, perhaps most notably health
spending. Reductions in cash benefits have been coupled with some increases in service outlays. These changes have been partially offsetting,
revealing a degree of inertia in the aggregated output of welfare states.

These developmental patterns raise a powerful question about the
mechanisms underlying overall persistence tendencies within welfare
states. Social policy stabilization, like patterns of change, requires explanation, and it poses a constructive challenge to welfare state theory (cf.
Pierson 2001b). Do the factors responsible for recent patterns of persistence differ from those behind the postwar expansion of welfare states?

Factors associated with mass opinion represent an important source of
welfare state persistence, but ones that have to this point been murky and

poorly defined. Aggregate opinion within developed democracies tends to
be characterized by a high degree of inertia or stability, in spite of a generation of concerted attacks on social provision from the political right. In
chapter 5, we examine this puzzle in more detail. For now, we emphasize
that because of this stability, mass policy preferences have tended to *constrain* more extensive shifts in the recent development of welfare states.

The results of our analyses in this chapter are much in keeping with this
proposition. In particular, our simulations suggest that more extensive patterns of ideological change would have decisively influenced the trajectory
of welfare state development within the politics on which we have focused.
Taking Norway as an exemplar of social democracies, a movement toward
the U.S. level of policy preferences would probably have transformed a
case of high and fairly stable welfare state effort into one of full-blown
retrenchment. We find similar results for Italy and Germany, where simulation of a trend toward American policy preferences transforms the baseline one-percentage-point increase in spending effort into a four-point net
decline in the Christian-democratic welfare state.

Regarding liberal democracies, our simulation results suggest that historical trends in policy preferences could have wielded significant influence over the recent evolution of liberal welfare states. For instance, a
movement in the United States toward the Norwegian level of policy preferences is, by itself, predicted as adding a sizable six percentage points to
the American level of welfare effort during the 1990s.

In thinking about the larger implications of these findings, we emphasize that mass policy preferences do not operate to the exclusion of other
causal factors. Our simulations also focused on two other large sources
of welfare state output: women's labor force participation and economic
development level. Changing the levels of either of these key factors influences the degree of welfare state spending relative to GDP. But the
consistently large effects in our temporal simulations involving mass policy preferences are thematically notable. In general, high levels of welfare
preference in much of Europe and *lower* levels of such preferences elsewhere contribute to a degree of stability and inertia within specific countries and ideal-typical regimes. A systematic focus on mass policy preferences helps to unpack the black box of persistence tendencies within
contemporary welfare states.

This extension of our embedded preferences approach shows points of
complementarity with path dependency theorizing. Pierson's (1996) path
dependency thesis identifies the asymmetric distribution of costs and ben-

CHAPTER FOUR

The Question of Convergence

With accumulating evidence casting doubt on forecasts of imminent decline in welfare states, some recent scholarship has instead focused on a different scenario: the prospects for cross-national *convergence*. Predictions that welfare states are becoming more similar over time, perhaps even converging on a common model of public provision, have long been present in the welfare state literature. This prediction, for example, was implicit in the logic of industrialism's focus on developmental processes that were assumed to operate similarly within industrial capitalism (Kerr, Dunlop, Harbinson, and Myers 1960; Cutright 1965, 1967; Form 1979). But the convergence hypothesis has recently been given a vigorous and more comprehensive reformulation by one of the founding figures of comparative welfare state research (Wilensky 2002). Convergence is also hypothesized in the global governance literature, especially a line of scholarship focused on the impact of the European Union (Kosenen 1995; Greve 1996; Scharpf 1997).

Arguments for convergence thus suggest another important line of debate among welfare state analysts (e.g., Esping-Andersen 1996a:4–5; Kautto et al. 2001a; Korpi 2003: 604). Indeed, much established welfare state theorizing continues to be premised on the existence of robust cross-national differences. For instance, the clustering of welfare states into enduring regime types is central to the power resources paradigm. Our embedded preferences thesis also anticipates significant—and persisting—welfare state differences, although we locate cross-national variation in contrasting patterns of aggregate policy preferences among national publics.

Have welfare states become more similar in the contemporary historical era? What factors generate convergence pressures, and what factors promote dissimilarity and divergence? We address these questions in this chapter. Our analyses build from the research design developed in the previous chapter, focusing on the historical period from 1980 through 2001. Given the possibility that contemporary trends originated during an earlier era, we also supplement our analysis of welfare state differences by using the more limited social security transfers measure for the earlier period from 1960 through 1980.

Perspectives on Welfare State Convergence

The New Modernization Thesis

An important, if rarely acknowledged, intellectual legacy of modernization theorizing is a focus on economic and demographic correlates of social policy development. This legacy is apparent in the scholarly focus on factors such as fiscal crisis and population aging as sources of historical pressures affecting developed welfare states (e.g., Kosenen 1995; Bonoli, George, and Taylor-Gooby 2000; Korpi 2003). These pressures also figure in the recent manifesto *Why We Need a New Welfare State* (2002). There, Esping-Andersen and his colleagues argue that a new synthetic model of social policy better balances the service-related needs of demographic groups such as women and immigrants with the goals of full employment and sustainable economic growth.

Of course, what distinguishes the use of demographic and economic arguments by power-resources and other scholars is the greater priority they attach to forces that inhibit retrenchment or convergence. But if economic and demographic factors are given greater weight as sources of future direction, we arrive at a perspective that resembles the modernization paradigm. This is precisely the position that has been recently articulated by one of the founding figures in the field of welfare state research, Harold Wilensky (2002).

Wilensky's central thesis is that economic change in the postwar era and in recent decades has exerted pressure for similar patterns of social policy development. As he puts it the opening pages of his recent book *Rich Democracies* (2002:3), "convergence theory is the idea that as rich countries got richer, they developed similar economic, political, and social structures . . ." But what distinguishes Wilensky's new paradigm from earlier modernization approaches is its explicit incorporation of political factors established by subsequent welfare state theorizing. This includes the power resources focus on political party conflict and the institutionalist/path dependency focus on constitutional structures. Indeed, Wilensky explicitly describes his research design as using convergence theory to explain similar developmental tendencies in affluent democracies, while resorting to political and institutional factors to explain away residual patterns of persisting differences.

Ultimately, however, it is convergence-inducing pressures that define the core of Wilensky's account, distinguishing it from currently dominant welfare state theories. Without resorting to the language of "functional prerequisites" found in the earlier logic of industrialism literature, he offers a probabilistic and vigorously asserted defense of one of the main expectations of the modernization paradigm. The key factor of economic development yields a surplus out of which public provisions can be funded, while also stimulating extensive demographic changes in family structure, gender roles, and population aging, where the latter exert strong pressures for new or more extensive social provisions (2002: chap. 1). In Wilensky's own words (2002: 214): "From 1980 to 1991, social spending grew in all 12 countries, but the differences between the less affluent countries and the most affluent declined. . . . The root cause of this general trend is economic growth and its demographic and bureaucratic outcomes."

This bold restatement of the modernization perspective deserves serious consideration. If true, it anticipates greater welfare state similarity over time, where this trend is assumed to be facilitated by the less-developed democracies (with smaller welfare states) catching up to the level of the richest democracies. Economic development processes, and also demographic change, are thus expected to be central mechanisms behind convergence tendencies. Our analyses consider these hypotheses in detail.

European Unification

A second potential source of welfare state convergence is the emergence of the European Union as a supranational organization with regulatory power over member countries (Greve 1996). In contrast to the domestic and *within-country* focus of Wilensky's new modernization paradigm, the EU argument identifies a novel *between-country* mechanism as stimulating convergence tendencies in European welfare states. According to this thesis, the growing administrative powers of the EU are expected to result in greater coordination among member nations, including with reference to welfare state policy.

Some analysts hypothesize that European Union influence over welfare states facilitates convergence by creating disincentives to high levels
of social provision (Kosenen 1995). In this context, the fiscal requirement
that EU members limit budget deficits to no more than 3 percent of GDP
may be a particularly important constraint on the high-spending welfare
states of northern Europe. As a source of convergence, we may expect that
the fiscal constraints of the European Union would become most apparent in the decade since the 1993 Maastricht Treaty formally established
current membership requirements.[1]

A second possibility is that establishment of the EU has increased the
probability that neoliberal policy ideas will diffuse to member nations. This
could involve the adoption of a more market-oriented approach to government regulation and spending. In this context, the absence of trans-
European political parties has been hypothesized as enhancing EU policy influence by limiting the ability of voters to challenge policy changes
through electoral means (Scharpf 1997).

To date, controversies surrounding the policy influence of the European Union have far exceeded the available evidence (Montanari 1995).
Some scholars have questioned whether the EU's half-century development has enabled governments within Western Europe to anticipate its
coming, thereby lessening any potential impacts (Kautto et al. 2001a, b).
By evaluating evidence for convergence involving welfare states within
social and Christian democracies, we examine the possibility that the development of the European Union has been a stimulus for convergence.

Why Might Differences Persist?

The core logic of power resources, path dependency, and institutional theories, and the embedded preferences approach, is generally at odds with
the scenario of welfare state convergence. Power resources analysts, for
instance, have acknowledged the existence of various global and transnational pressures on national governments, while asserting the inability of
these factors, as yet, to alter the fundamental attributes of welfare states
(Esping-Andersen 1996b). Nevertheless, power resources expectations
concerning persistent cross-national differences in policymaking apply
primarily to *regime types*, rather than to specific welfare states. Indeed,
within-regime differences involving specific countries are assumed to be
less extensive than *between*-regime differences. The United States and
Canada, for instance, should be more similar to each other with respect
to welfare state policymaking than to Sweden or Norway.

Recent extensions of power resources theory have hypothesized that regime types face distinct environmental pressures toward change (Esping-Andersen 1996b; Korpi and Palme 1998; Huber and Stephens 2001). While this may eventually lead to greater *within*-regime similarity, *between*-regime differences are predicted to continue or even to grow. We incorporate these claims in the analyses developed in this chapter by considering the variability over time between specific welfare states.

Our embedded preferences approach shares with power resources theory expectations about the persistence of different types of regimes, and thus long-term processes constraining tendencies toward convergence. The main difference is that our theory identifies mass policy preferences as a central mechanism underlying cross-national differences in welfare states. For convergence to occur, the policy preferences of different national publics would have to become considerably more similar over time. This would exert pressure toward the adoption of a more homogeneous approach to welfare policymaking across countries.

Given significant tendencies toward aggregate-level stability found in our ISSP/OECD dataset and with respect to comparative opinion research (e.g., Smith 1990b; Page and Shapiro 1992; Pettersen 1995; Svallfors 1995), our embedded preferences approach provides little grounds for expecting convergence trends in the contemporary historical era. However, it is premature to answer the question of convergence without further analysis, and the results we develop enable us to directly address this issue. Our multivariate analyses provide an additional perspective on the convergence scenario by investigating whether more extensive changes in policy preferences could have led to greater similarity in contemporary welfare states.

Analzying Convergence

Between-Country, Between-Regime, and Within-Regime Differences

Close examination reveals that controversies over convergence raise not one but three separate questions about welfare state variation over time. A full exploration of the convergence thesis requires us to address each in turn. The first concerns cross-national variation in welfare states, or, what we will refer to as *between-country* differences in welfare states. This type of cross-national variation is the primary focus of the new modernization theory. A second type of convergence involves the differences between welfare state regime types. Such *between-regime* differences are a primary focus of power resources theory, and evidence of convergence between regimes would thus yield a significant criticism of that theory. Finally, a third dimension of variation relates to *within-regime* differences among welfare states within a particular type of regime. It could be that differences between regimes remain large, yet there is convergence *within* regimes. Because these three types of variation in welfare states are analytically distinct, questions about convergence trends are usefully investigated in turn.

We measure the three types of welfare state differences by calculating the standard deviation for a set of observations on welfare states or types of regimes. Our *between-country* measure is the standard deviation of welfare state values for countries. Our *between-regime* measure is the standard deviation of regime-specific values, where the latter are the average for the countries composing a given regime type. Our *within-regime* measure is the standard deviation of values among countries within a specific type of regime. These standardized measures enable us to compare the degree of welfare state and regime-type variation over time, thereby gauging the evidence for trends involving similarities or differences in spending effort.[2]

Data

The data we analyze in this chapter are from the OECD and ISSP/OECD datasets introduced in chapters 2 and 3. The OECD dataset contains nearly complete information on overall welfare spending effort in eighteen developed democracies for the period from 1980 through 2001. We use these data to develop estimates of trends involving between-country, between-regime, and within-regime dimensions of welfare state variation. We then analyze the sources of welfare state variation using the merged ISSP/OECD dataset. These data allow us to develop estimates of the effects of change in mass policy preferences and other theoretically relevant factors on welfare state convergence and divergence.

Our analyses of welfare state variability focus primarily on the OECD social expenditures measure of overall welfare state effort for the contemporary historical era between 1980 and 2001. However, we also use the social security transfers measure that we introduced in chapter 3 to develop a supplemental analysis of trends in welfare state variation during the earlier historical era between 1960 and 1980. The social security transfers measure is, of course, a more restricted welfare state measure, generally excluding spending on public service provisions. However, as before, inclusion of this measure in the analysis permits us to guard against the possibility that convergence trends may have emerged in the historical era *prior* to 1980.

Independent Variables

The independent variables that we consider in this chapter are the same as those in chapters 2 and 3 (see tables 2.1, 2.2, and 3.1). The coefficients estimates with which we derive key predictions are from our statistical model of welfare effort. As before, this model uses robust-cluster standard errors to take into account the non-independence of errors in the analysis of country-level data.

The goal of the multivariate analyses we develop is to estimate the effects of change in the level of specific variables on predicted differences between welfare states and types of regimes. As discussed in greater detail below, we develop estimates of the effects on between-country/regime variation of change in per capita GDP, women's labor force participation, and mass policy preferences. These economic and demographic factors are useful indicators of the new modernization paradigm's focus, while policy preferences reflect our own theoretical focus. Complementing the analysis of observed trends, these estimates provide a perspective from which to better appreciate what factors could have generated more extensive patterns of convergence and/or divergence.

Between-Country and Between-Regime Differences

Are cross-national differences in welfare states since 1980 suggestive of convergence? Have differences between social, Christian, and liberal regimes experienced a similar pattern of change during this time? We address these questions using results of the analyses displayed in figure 4.1. Estimates in the left-hand panel of the figure are standard deviations in *countries'* observed level of welfare state effort for a given year. Estimates in the right-hand panel are standard deviations in *regimes'* observed level of welfare state effort (where countries have been aggregated into one of the three regime types). Note that because the data series for Austria and Norway are much shorter than for other OECD democracies, we present measures using both a "long" series (excluding Austria and Norway) and

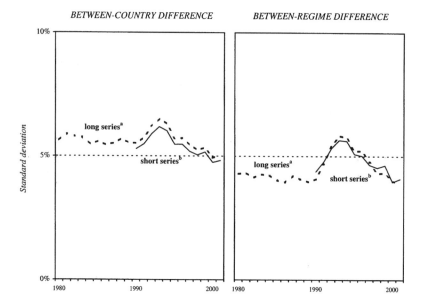

FIGURE 4.1. Trends in between-country and between-regime differences in welfare state effort, 1980–2001; a. long series excludes Austria and Norway.; b. short series = Austria, Australia, Belgium, Canada, Denmark, Finland, France, Germany, Ireland, Italy, Japan, Netherlands, New Zealand, Norway, Spain, Sweden, Switzerland, United Kingdom., and United States

a "short" series (including Austria and Norway) in each of the figure's panels.

Starting with the left-hand panel, our measure of between-country differences in welfare state effort shows some variation over time and a modest net reduction in both the long and short series. In the long series, the magnitude of this decline is on the order of 10 percent, from an initial standard deviation value of .056 in 1980 to a value of .05 in 2001. The magnitude of this decline is comparable in the short series, where the initial index value in 1990 is .053 and the corresponding value for 2001 is .048. The average index value of roughly .05 in both series implies a substantial degree of variation in welfare states, with the typical difference between the overall spending of the two OECD countries being ten percentage points in a given year.

Turning to the right-hand panel, welfare *regime* differences increased in the early 1990s, moving back subsequently to levels found during the 1980s. The inverted-U-shaped pattern of change in between-regime differences is similar to the over-time pattern for between-country differences. But whereas between-country differences declined by approximately 10 percent in magnitude, the net change in between-regime differences is a bit smaller, approximately 7 percent in both the long and short series.

What evidence is there for convergence trends occurring prior to 1980–2001, particularly in view of the earlier logic of industrialism argument? In figure 4.2, we examine this question by considering between-country and between-regime differences during the twenty-year period from 1960 through 1980. We use the same standard deviation measure, but it is calculated for the OECD's social security transfers data available during this earlier time period.

Results for the social security transfers data show a steady increase in between-country and between-regime differences between 1960 and 1980. These results complement the analyses presented in chapter 3. They reveal that the pattern of welfare state expansion shared by developed democracies during this time was also accompanied by rising cross-national and between-regime differences. These results extend our analysis of cross-national differences during the period 1980 through 2001. They provide evidence against an earlier trend involving welfare state convergence.

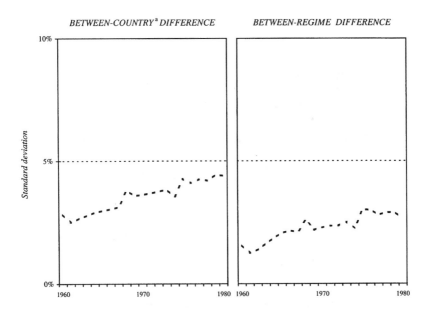

FIGURE 4.2. Trends in between-country and between-regime differences in social security transfers, 1960–1980: a. Countries = Austria, Australia, Canada, Denmark, Finland, France, Germany, Ireland, Italy, Japan, Netherlands, New Zealand, Norway, Sweden, Switzerland, United Kingdom, and United States

Within-Regime Differences

What of the pattern of *within*-regime differences? We present results of these analyses in figure 4.3. The three sets of calculations show differences in welfare state spending within social, Christian, and liberal democracies. In 1990, the deviation from the mean among Christian democracies (Austria, Belgium, France, Germany, Italy, Netherlands, Spain, and Switzerland) was 3.3 percentage points. By 1994, this value had decreased to 2.5 percent, subsequently stabilizing during the remainder of the decade.

Welfare state differences within social democracies also experienced a large decline (–22%) during this time, moving from approximately three percentage points in the late 1980s to 2.4 percent in 2001. The time series

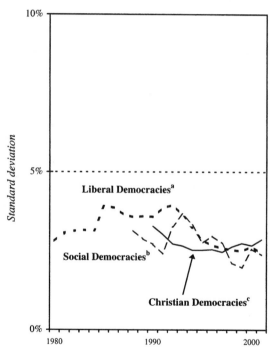

WITHIN-REGIME DIFFERENCE

FIGURE 4.3. Trends in within-regime differences in welfare state effort, 1980–2001: a. Australia, Canada, Ireland, New Zealand, United Kingdom, and United States; b. Denmark, Finland, Norway, and Sweden; c. Austria, Belgium, France, Germany, Italy, Netherlands, Spain, and Switzerland.

for liberal democracies shows a net decline between 1980 (2.8) and 2001 (2.4). If we focus on the period between the late 1980s and 2001 so as to make more comparisons with the shorter series for social and Christian democracies, we find a much higher rate of decline in within-regime differences among liberal democracies.

This evidence for the growing similarity of welfare state spending output among countries comprised by a specific regime type is noteworthy. It tells us that welfare states classified *within* the same type of regime have become more similar to one another over time. This finding is usefully juxtaposed with the results of our between-country and between-regime analyses. Recall that the key finding there concerned a noticeable, if modest, decline in between-country differences in welfare state effort, with between-regime differences showing a smaller contraction. From the perspective of our within-regime results, we can now see that the modest trend toward greater cross-national similarity in welfare states is largely a product of countries with similar types of welfare states coming to resemble each other more. A final result from the OECD data is in order. Here we consider the picture of between-regime trends that emerges when we focus on the single contrast between social/Christian versus liberal democracies. In other words, we now treat the social/Christian regimes as one single type for purposes of comparison. We present in figure 4.4 standardized differences for liberal welfare states (including Ireland and the United Kingdom) versus European welfare states (social and Christian democracies).

The average difference between liberal versus European welfare states increased between the 1980s and early 1990s, moving from 3.5 percentage points in 1980 to approximately 4.0 by the mid-1990s. Results using the shorter series do not, in this case, allow us to observe the lower levels of variability during the 1980s. But using the data in the longer series, this modest trend toward polarization of the two aggregated types of welfare regimes is both important and unexpected. We discuss implications in greater detail in the chapter's conclusions. For now, we emphasize that this provides additional evidence of persisting or increasing differences between welfare regimes.

Sources of Welfare State Convergence and Divergence

What causal factors promote convergence or divergence among welfare states? This question is an important one for welfare state theory, par-

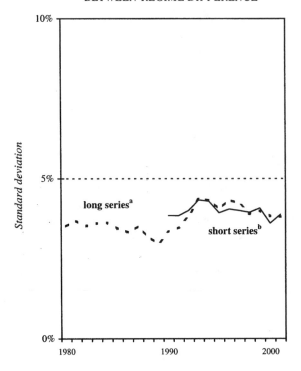

BETWEEN-REGIME DIFFERENCE

FIGURE 4.4. Trends in social/Christian vs. liberal differences in welfare state effort, 1980–2001; a. long series excludes Austria and Norway.; b. short series = Austria, Australia, Belgium, Canada, Denmark, Finland, France, Germany, Ireland, Italy, Japan, Netherlands, New Zealand, Norway, Spain, Sweden, Switzerland, United Kingdom, and United States

ticularly because the convergence trends we have unearthed have been modest in size, and concentrated primarily within regime types.

The multivariate analyses presented in table 4.1 yield answers to this question. Estimates in this table are standardized differences in welfare effort for social, Christian, and liberal democracies in 1991 and 1997. The standard deviation calculation is the same as in the earlier analysis presented in figure 4.1, but the current values for the three regimes are estimates derived from our statistical model of the merged ISSP/OECD dataset. The first set of estimates is the baseline prediction, and it reflects no manipulation of covariates in our statistical model, providing a point of comparison for our subsequent estimates. Estimates 2 through 5 are derived by adjusting, respectively, the level of a single, theoretically relevant covariate to obtain regime-specific predictions. We then used these predictions, in turn, to calculate new estimates of regime differences.

Our second set of estimates shows that a movement during the 1990s to the U.S. level of economic development does not alter the between-regime variability established by the baseline estimate. But our third set of estimates for a movement to the Norwegian level of women's labor-force participation enhances the baseline trend. Their estimate provides evidence that trends involving a substantial shift in women's labor force participation would likely have generated new divergence pressures on welfare regimes.

Turning to mass policy preferences, however, the fourth set of estimates in table 4.1 identifies a large source of potential regime convergence. More specifically, under the assumption that all three regime types adopt the U.S. level of policy preferences, fully half of the predicted regime differences in welfare state effort disappear in 1997. In estimate 5, the effect of regimes moving to the Norwegian level of policy preferences is also quite large, transforming the baseline rise in regime differences into a decrease during the 1990s.

How might our results change if we consider *two* regime types, rather than three, thereby classifying social and Christian democracies as a single European regime? The results presented in table 4.2 for this two-regime analysis of liberal versus European welfare states are quite similar to the findings for our three-regime comparison. A movement by both regime types to the U.S. level of economic development leaves trends in between-regime differences unchanged (estimate 2). But a demographic transition involving trends toward the Norwegian level of women's labor force participation (estimate 3) generates larger regime differences. In estimate 4, the predicted effects of a common movement to the U.S. level of policy

TABLE 4.1   **Predicted Between-Regime Differences in Welfare State Effort**

Regimes	1991	1997
Social, Christian, and liberal democracies		
1. Baseline prediction	4%	5%
2. Economic development (*high*[a])	4%	5%
3. Women's labor force participation (*high*[b])	4%	6%
4. Policy preferences (*low*[c])	4%	2%
5. Policy preferences (*high*[d])	4%	3%

[a]U.S. level of per capita GDP.
[b]Norwegian level of women's labor force participation.
[c]U.S. level of mass policy preferences.
[d]Norwegian level of mass policy preferences.

preferences are again considerable, eliminating nearly half of between-regime differences. A trend toward the Norwegian level of policy preferences generates more modest convergence pressures in the final estimate.

The remaining estimates shown in table 4.2 are for analyzing *between-country* differences among the five democracies (Australia, Germany, Italy, Norway, and the United States) for which we have complete data in 1991 and 1997. The between-country results for our estimates of economic development (estimate 2), women's labor force participation (estimate 3), and anti-welfare opinion trends (estimate 5) are comparable to the earlier results. Trends toward the Norwegian level of policy preferences (estimate 4) yield a different conclusion, for they generate much more modest convergence pressures. Overall, then, the general pattern of results for between-country welfare state differences is comparable to those found for regime-based differences.

Rethinking the Convergence Thesis

Our point of departure in this chapter has been the possibility that welfare states within developed democracies have become more similar to one another over time, converging upon a common level of expenditure or social provision (Kosenen 1995; Greve 1996; Wilensky 2002). Scholarly debates during the past two decades have focused primarily on evidence concern-

TABLE 4.2   **Predicted Between-Regime and Between-Country Differences in Welfare State Effort**

Regimes/Countries	1991	1997
Social/Christian versus liberal democracies		
1. Baseline prediction	4%	5%
2. Economic development (*high*[a])	4%	5%
3. Women's labor force participation (*high*[b])	4%	6%
4. Policy preferences (*low*[c])	4%	2%
5. Policy preferences (*high*[d])	4%	4%
All democracies		
1. Baseline prediction	4%	6%
2. Economic development (*high*[a])	4%	6%
3. Women's labor force participation (*high*[b])	4%	6%
4. Policy preferences (*low*[c])	4%	4%
5. Policy preferences (*high*[d])	4%	4%

[a]U.S. level of per capita GDP.
[b]Norwegian level of women's labor force participation.
[c]U.S. level of mass policy preferences.
[d]Norwegian level of mass policy preferences.

ing welfare state retrenchment, but convergence represents an analytically distinct and important scenario. Indeed, if convergence has occurred, it would call into question welfare state theories predicated upon the existence of extensive cross-national variation. In keeping with the centrality of the themes relating to "varieties of capitalism" (Hall and Soskice 2001) and "worlds" of welfare regimes (Esping-Andersen 1990), this would encompass the dominant theoretical approaches developed since the modernization theories of the 1960s.

Starting with the question of *between-country* differences in welfare states, we find evidence for a modest decline in cross-national variability in welfare effort during the 1980–2001 era. By the same token, however, the actual magnitude of this decline is as yet modest, with recent levels of welfare state variability retaining 90 percent of their earlier levels from the 1980s. In 2001, the average difference in spending effort between a given pair of OECD democracies was a sizable ten percentage points.

Our parallel analysis of *between-regime* differences in welfare state regime types provides less evidence of a net decline in variability. The average difference between social, Christian, and liberal democratic regimes retained 93 percent of its earlier magnitude. By itself, this result cast doubt on forecasts of the merging of social, Christian, and liberal democratic states into a single type of regime.

But consideration of the third dimension of *within-regime* variation sheds perhaps the most telling light on trends in welfare state variability. Here, our key result is that the welfare states within each regime type have come to more closely resemble their fellow members. To put this finding another way, Christian democratic welfare states were more similar to one another by the end of the 1980–2001 period, and the same is true for liberal and social democratic welfare states.

What this means is that the modest degree of cross-national convergence trends involving specific welfare states is mostly a product of growing *within-regime similarity*. We corroborated this point by recalculating the trends in between-regime variability for liberal welfare states versus social/Christian democracies. These analyses provided evidence for substantial and persisting between-regime differences during the 1990s, where the latter were slightly larger than in the earlier decade of the 1980s.

With respect to European welfare states, evidence for a degree of growing similarity is clearly notable, particularly in light of the thesis of European Union effects on members' welfare states. Upon closer inspection, however, the trend we have discovered runs contrary to the European

Union version of the convergence scenario in which a fiscally constraining regional association forces members to adopt *lower* levels of welfare expenditure. The poor fit between the EU-driven convergence model and our results is especially clear for the post-Maastricht era since 1993. For it is this historical period that convergence theories anticipate as a crucible in which high-spending European governments have been forced to make programmatic cuts in social spending and public entitlements. To this point, then, the maturation of the European Union appears compatible with the maintenance of generous welfare states.

Sources of Convergence versus Divergence in Welfare States

How does Wilensky's bold reformulation of the modernization paradigm fare in light of this chapter's findings? With respect to trends in welfare state variability, there is little clear evidence that convergence will occur as less-developed countries experience economic development, fueling demographic change and welfare state expansion. While the continental Christian democracies have lower levels of economic development than the social democracies, so too do liberal democracies, with the exception of Japan and the United States. But as we have seen, modest trends involving growing cross-national similarity are primarily due to regimes becoming more internally homogeneous. Liberal and social democracies became more distinct from one another during the 1990s.

Clearly, the focus of the modernization approach on demographic factors has merit. Our multivariate analyses of women's labor force participation do not provide evidence of *convergence* pressures. Indeed, our use of deliberately large trends in the levels of economic and demographic variables led to predictions that left intact or even increased the majority of differences between welfare state regimes.

Our evidence suggests that policy preferences represent the consistently *largest* source of diversity and variability between welfare states. In particular, it is the typically higher level of policy preferences in social and Christian democracies in comparison to liberal democracies that continues to underlie much of cross-national differences in welfare state effort. It is thus critical to consider—once again—the relevance of citizens' preferences in gauging the current and future diversity among welfare states among the developed democracies.

CHAPTER FIVE

Where Do Welfare State Preferences Come From?

The results presented in the last three chapters compel an affirmative response to the overarching question of this book: mass policy preferences do indeed represent a major source of influence on the policy activities of contemporary welfare states. Mass preferences are a key factor behind cross-national differences in social spending, and they exert significant constraint on retrenchment pressures. These findings now lead us to an important new question: What are the origins of citizens' preferences relating to welfare states? This is an essential question for empirical democratic theory as well as for our investigations of welfare states.

In recent years, a number of scholars have embraced an "economic" perspective to understand the origins of voters' policy preferences, identifying changes in the macroeconomy, and voters' responses to such changes, as dominant factors. This approach is fundamentally indebted to Anthony Downs's *An Economic Theory of Democracy* (1957). It has also been influential in recent opinion/policy research.

In the work of Wlezien and Soroka (Wlezien 1995, 1996, 2004; Soroka and Wlezien 2004a, 2005), for example, national publics are expected to respond rapidly to changes in the macroeconomic environment and with respect to past policies. This means that individuals, and in turn the aggregate public, continually update their preferences, exerting pressure on politicians' decision-making and the outputs of government. Because these relationships involve mutual adjustment on the part of citizens and government officials, Wlezien and Soroka capture mass opinion with the metaphor of a thermostat. This suggests a portrait of mass policy preferences as unsettled, even volatile in the face of yearly policy changes, as well as fluctuations in the business cycle.

The economic approach is not the only possible perspective on causal factors of mass policy preferences. In the history of survey research on mass opinion in democracies, a second set of insights leads toward the embedded preferences approach that we introduced in chapter 1. Contrasting with the economic approach, the embedded preferences approach is causally inclusive, identifying multiple social factors behind mass policy attitudes, and not solely economic processes. These include individuals' location within class and social structure, participation in or proximity to major social institutions, and the historical influence of state-making and national development (e.g., Lipset 1981; Manza and Brooks 1999; Brooks 2006). These factors have a centrally distinguishing feature: because they tend to change slowly over time, their operation as a source of influence over policy preferences can lend a degree of stability or inertia to the ongoing evolution of attitudes.

We believe the embedded preferences approach enables insights into precisely this feature of welfare state preferences, namely, their slow-moving pattern of change. Indeed, whereas the economic approach predicts considerable volatility in aggregate preferences, even over relatively short periods of time, the embedded preferences approach anticipates inertia. This line of thinking does not mean that economic factors are irrelevant—only that they are not necessarily the sole or even primary foundation of mass policy preferences. The distribution of social and institutional factors changes more slowly than do economic variables, dampening volatility in welfare state preferences.

In addressing the question of origins, our goal in this chapter is to articulate and apply a sociologically informed approach more centrally to the study of welfare state attitudes. We do so by first identifying key points of constructive difference between the two general approaches. We analyze survey data for four countries to evaluate expectations about the structure and sources of policy preferences concerning the welfare state.

Two Models of Policy Preferences

The Economic Approach

Economic approaches start from the assumption that mass policy preferences are an outcome of individuals' calculations of expected benefits, where "streams of utility" are influenced by changes in both the economy and the policy activities of government (Downs 1957). Individuals, and in the aggregate, the entire polity, form policy attitudes on the basis of calculations of self-interest.[1] Economic models are further distinguished in assuming not only self-interested attitudes, but also that individuals are best understood as having maximizing dispositions that lead to frequent updating of their preferences.[2]

What implications does the economic approach have when applied to the study of welfare state preferences? In a nutshell, while *negative* economic expectations provide individuals with a reason to support government provision, *positive* expectations provide less grounds for supporting high levels of social spending. In short, citizens are committed to ideas about policy and government only to the extent that their current economic circumstances provide a compelling reason.

By the same token, individuals face significant limits in their capacity to obtain information and make forecasts, especially when we consider ordinary voters and mass opinion in the aggregate. How, then, is economically motivated opinion formation possible? In this context, a notable contribution to economic models of opinion has been to incorporate—from cognitive psychology—the idea that "heuristic" decision-making effectively compensates for low levels of information.[3] Low levels of economic information can, for instance, result in individuals relying upon (perceptions of) past economic performance to make future predictions and thus evaluate their degree of support for various public policy options (Fiorina 1981). A second heuristic that has been widely employed by proponents of the economic approach is *sociotropic* evaluation, whereby individuals take into account the performance of the national economy, and not merely their own personal economic circumstances (Kiewiet 1983).

Applications of the economic approach to policy preferences have been popular in research on opinion/policy linkages. For Wlezien, aggregate opinion and public policy have a "thermostatic" relationship, in which public policy is influenced by mass opinion *and* mass opinion is shaped by previous levels of policy output (Wlezien 1995; see also Soroka and Wlezien 2004). As a result, aggregate opinion is expected to follow a pattern of "pronounced cyclicality" over time (Wlezien 1995:99). Growth in government spending leads to lower public support for government policy, while low levels of spending stimulate greater public preference for government involvement. According to Wlezien, this is true within specific policy domains and government output as a whole. In recent and innovative work, Soroka and Wlezien (2004) use country-specific data on budgetary appropriations and expenditures to examine how opinion and policy adjust to each other within Canada, the United Kingdom, and the United States.

The comprehensive scholarship of Erikson, MacKuen, and Stimson

(2002a, b; see also Stimson 1991, 2004) shares a key feature of the economic approach in its thesis that American policy preferences are formed in response to changes in the national economy and the policy activities of government. Erikson et al. (2002a: xviii) invoke the economic model's assumption that in the aggregate individuals are maximizers who update their preferences continually, so that "the real aggregate is quite nimble, changing its partisan balance in response, for example, to real economic indicators of the last quarter." It should be emphasized that Erikson, Mac-Kuen, and Stimson (and Wlezien) do not argue against the operation of *other* factors behind the formation of mass policy preferences, or that *some* types of policy preferences may be less responsive to economic change. In principle, there is room for propositions to this effect.

In Erikson and colleagues' (2002a, chap. 4) discussion of mass opinion "mood," one of the more notable themes is that aggregate opinion is inherently unsettled. A significant portion of Erikson et al.'s empirical analyses is geared toward establishing the malleability of American policy preferences in the face of even relatively small changes in government policies or the economy. Erikson et al. argue (2002a: chap. 9) that the influence of past government policies on aggregate opinion occurs almost instantaneously, even more rapidly than the policy responsiveness of government officials to prior changes in mass opinion.[4] The concluding chapter of *The Macro Polity* (2002a: chap. 10) proposes a systems theory in which public opinion moves in relation to policy: when policy becomes more liberal, opinion pushes it back to the center, and vice versa if policy moves too far in a conservative direction.

The Embedded Preferences Approach

The core of the economic model of policy preferences rests on a view of individuals as disposed to modify their policy preferences in light of on-going patterns of change in the economy and/or government policy. Our alternative view emphasizes the embeddedness of individuals and their attitudes in social relations and contexts. The key idea is that individuals' social locations impose limits on the malleability of policy preferences. Dynamic economic influences may be present, but powerful social factors tend to constrain attitude shifts among individuals, and in the aggregate. *Who* people are matters for their policy attitudes, and individuals' social identities, for example, as professionals, immigrants, observant Catholics, or Swedes—are not wholly remade in the face of fluctuations in the business cycle.

We identify three main sources of social influence over mass policy attitudes: (1) interests individuals have by virtue of social-structural locations; (2) participation in discursive communities that are characteristic of such major institutions as churches and schools; and (3) long-term patterns involving the influence of welfare state-making itself, where these operate through collective memory processes. The tendency of the distribution and effects of these three types of social factors to change slowly over time frequently confers on mass opinion a degree of inertia in the aggregate. The divergence between a model of individuals as continually updating their preferences and one of acting on socially embedded identities has implications for understanding patterns of change over time in welfare state attitudes.

The sociological thinking behind our embedded preferences approach originated in early investigations of policy attitudes within democracies. Social-structural factors behind the distribution of policy preferences were analyzed, for example, in Lipset's (1981 [1960]) pioneering comparative research on the development of social cleavages. Countering orthodox Marxist interpretations, Lipset argued that the existence of multiple and cross-cutting social cleavages tended to routinize ideological conflict, enhancing the legitimacy of postwar democratic capitalism. A key assumption was that material or economic risks were themselves filtered through the social locations of individuals; economic change or crisis, by itself, would be insufficient to fully dislodge the stakes individuals were assumed to have in existing institutions and social arrangements.[5] This was important with respect to such key groups as the new middle classes, whose relative size and partisan political alignments were viewed by Lipset as critical to the emergence and stability of democratic societies.[6]

The operation of institutional factors can be appreciated in groundbreaking research conducted by Stouffer (1992[1955]) on the sources of democratic tolerance. Stouffer argued that Americans' willingness to support civil liberties for members of controversial groups was a product of several distinct factors: generation-specific exposure to more- versus less-restrictive political environments; individuals' degree of experience with the liberalizing effects of education; and residential location in urban versus less-cosmopolitan residential locations. Rather than reflecting economically malleable preferences, an essential assumption of this research is that civil liberties attitudes are grounded in socially meaningful communities that carry with them distinctive and at times conflicting views of civil society and public policy. One of Stouffer's notable predictions was that the replacement of older by younger generations, when coupled with the steady increase of educational achievement in the United States, provided a foundation for subsequent growth in mass support for civil liberties.[7] Educational institutions promulgate a distinctive view of the world, one whose relevance extends to the formation of policy attitudes, including with reference to greater toleration of dissenting speech and other aspects of civil liberties.[8]

Assumptions that individuals' policy preferences are shaped by their locations in social structures *and* major institutions are central to contemporary applications of the sociological model of political behavior (Manza and Brooks 1999). Regular participation in social institutions exposes members to dominant or challenger political cultures, holding constant their social-structural locations. For example, in recent years a growing body of work has focused on religious organizations and networks as sources of policy preferences (e.g., Woodberry and Smith 1998; Sherkat and Ellison 1999; Brooks 2002), arguing that such communities disseminate religious doctrines that have significant ideological content. Such patterns of influence are notable in that they tend to reflect not only social inequalities between religious groups, but also normative imperatives that stem from theology and competing ideas of relevance to policymaking. From this perspective, religious processes influence individuals by affecting their degree of proximity to competing ideas of collective identity and public policy (see also McClosky and Zaller 1984; Lipset 1996). This notion also readily applies to participation in other major social institutions and organizations, such as unions, political parties, and schools and universities, as well as households/families (see, e.g., Verba, Schlozman, and Brady 1996; Burns, Schlozman, and Verba 2001). Major organizations and institutions typically exhibit a significant degree of stability with respect to the ideas and outlooks around which they are organized. Churches, schools, communities, workplaces, and other such settings influence the individuals who participate in them. This in turn contributes to *aggregate* stability in mass opinion.

To be sure, institutions and organizations are subject to constant historical pressures. For instance, if opinion leaders within a major institution embrace a novel outlook or doctrine relevant to policy attitudes, its diffusion to members has potentially profound consequences. Further, because individuals are situated in overlapping institutions and social networks, developments in one location can spread to influence nonmembers as well (Mutz 2006). One such example is the transition from authoritarian to democratic governance that has unfolded around the world over the past two decades (see also Lijphart 1994, 1999). Such institutionally based transformations are generally rare, and their occurrence usually signifies dramatic social and political change. Most of the time, on a day-to-day or even a year-to-year basis, institutional inertia rather than transformation is the hallmark of social organization.

A third set of factors that has received increasing attention in recent years concerns citizens' *collective memories*. Collective-memory scholars have assembled a rich array of evidence concerning the ways in which the historical past, particularly as regards episodes of state-making and policy conflict, comes to be viewed through the lens of assumptions concerning the identity and trajectory of a nation.[9] These assumptions, in turn, help to shape a national public's attitudes toward government, and their expectations regarding politicians and policies.

Collective-memory processes are decidedly not neutral. They convey normative judgments of specific events, individuals, or institutions. In this way, collective memory is frequently a vehicle for nationalism, where a country's leaders or founding principles are often seen as having the essential, even transcendental, importance for citizens (Gillis 1996). Constitutional revolutions and instances of state-making provide much of the content of collective memory within a specific nation. It is notable that these themes are often depicted in a stylized fashion (Brubaker 1996; Lipset 1996), lending them clarity and emotional salience in the minds of individuals.

While collective-memory scholars have not focused their work on social policy development per se, two key themes of this literature fit well with our embedded preferences approach to policy attitudes. The first of these concerns the content of collective memory, where a focus on past wars, political leaders, and episodes of political scandal is usefully complemented by further perspective on the making of welfare states. We expect, in particular, that citizens' level of preference for public versus private social provision is influenced by historical narratives about the degree to which efforts at developing public provision arrangements have proven successful. Indeed, in line with recent commentaries on welfare state legitimacy (Korpi and Palme 1998; Rothstein 1998), the establishment of *universalistic* regimes foreshadows their high levels of subsequent popularity, for the collective memories that tend to arise within these regimes have been quite favorable in tone. In contrast, welfare states that are vulnerable to partisan criticism or full-blown retrenchment tend to elicit lower public support. The narratives they have inspired are frequently more negative, invoking fewer symbols of national pride or necessity, while also generating higher levels of resentment of welfare recipients (Gilens 1999; Pierson 2001b; Larsen 2006).

The second theme we extract from the literature concerns the tendency for collective-memory narratives to persist over time. Once established, they become the baseline for further developments. One key reason is cognitive: collective memory is itself an instance of satisficing, where simplification rather than historical complexity operates (Schudson 1992). A further reason lies with the affective content of collective memories, where historical narratives tend to build from robust patterns of emotional identification and response (Olick 1999a). To be sure, changing historical events or sponsorship of collective-memory narratives can and do result in significant modifications or even reversals, as Schwartz's research on changing interpretations of Abraham Lincoln suggests (2000; see also Schwartz and Schuman 2005). Nevertheless, in developed countries, a degree of continuity in collective memory is more common than fluctuation or substantial change, at least over relatively short periods of time of several years or a decade or two. This is because collective memory is frequently reinforced and affirmed through a variety of artifacts and documents, as well as celebrations or rituals, many of which are officially endorsed or diffused by national government (Gillis 1996).

The temporal dimensions of collective memory are, then, much in keeping with expectations concerning inertia in mass preferences. But we also emphasize the divergence between collective memories of welfare state development and *contemporaneous* patterns of policy feedback. The latter type of feedback is short-term, where citizens are expected to respond instantaneously to current levels of policy output. In contrast, collective memories of welfare state development involve a much longer form of policy feedback, stretching back in historical time. Applied to welfare states, collective memories can of course be modified, but this takes time, as the legacies of earlier developments must first be displaced.

Implications for Understanding Welfare State Preferences

The embedded preferences approach to policy preferences implies predictions and explanatory propositions that diverge from those of the economic model. Rather than cyclical trends or extensive short-term fluctuation, our sociological model anticipates greater stability, and when aggregate opinion shifts, it will usually involve monotonic patterns of change that unfold over longer periods of time. Where the economic model identifies shifts in public policy direction or economic trends as responsible for trends in aggregate policy preferences, the embedded preferences approach identifies a greater plurality of factors, including (slower) changes in social structure and major institutions. Finally, the economic model implies that economic factors should have a considerably larger influence over the policy preferences of individuals than will social and institutional factors.

These three considerations—short-term fluctuation versus longer-run stability, shifts in economic factors versus a plurality of factors in accounting for change over time, and the relative importance of economic factors and noneconomic factors as sources of individuals' policy preferences—identify key points of divergence between the embedded preferences and economic models. Indeed, they establish what amounts to competing hypotheses about the empirical evidence concerning welfare state preferences. In the remainder of this chapter, we consider the evidence for each.

Data and Measures for Evaluating Approaches

Our first comparison of the two models considers the structure of change in aggregate policy preferences. As we have noted, the economic model implies a pattern of extensive short-term fluctuation. In contrast, our alternative approach anticipates a pattern of greater stability and monotonic trends in aggregate policy preferences.

Our second test evaluates the economic model's key explanatory proposition by analyzing regression models of policy preferences that take into account economic evaluations. While our statistical models include indicators of social factors, the main goal of this second test is to evaluate the empirical adequacy of the economic model by introducing respondents' economic evaluations. The expectation is that shifts in economic evaluations should be closely related to patterns of aggregate change in policy preferences.

Our third set of analyses compares the relative contributions of economic evaluations versus social factors to understanding the origins of individuals' policy preferences. Data limitations restrict our analysis to institutional and social-structural factors that are measurable in the country-specific surveys that we analyze. However, as will become apparent in the course of the analyses, our results provide a consistent portrait of mass policy preferences that bears on predictions offered by the two approaches.

We emphasize that the analysis in this chapter uses individual-level data from national surveys. Our reliance on survey data is deliberate. There are three main reasons behind this individual-level analysis. First, the theories that we address have clear behavioral implications. They suggest diverging hypotheses concerning the origins of individuals' policy attitudes and the relative impact of exposure to social and economic factors. Individual-level analyses enable us to directly measure the key theoretical concepts of economic evaluations and policy preferences. These are critical in light of the subjective nature of economic factors.[10]

A second reason for analyzing survey data is the absence of a compelling reason to treat economic evaluations as purely aggregate-level phenomena. This contrasts fundamentally with the setup of our cross-sectional time-series analyses, where the linkage between policy preferences and policy output occurs solely at the aggregate level. Political officials encounter policy attitudes in the *aggregate*. In this chapter, however, our interest is in the underlying sources of aggregate preferences. Hence, in contrast to our earlier analyses, we must analyze policy preferences and economic evaluations using survey data for individuals.

A final benefit of individual-level analysis is that country-level analysis of the relationship between economic factors and policy preferences risks ecological inference bias. This is particularly important in light of evidence that has accumulated in the years since Kramer's (1983) argument for restricting the study of economic voting to aggregate-level analysis. Attempting to analyze the impact of macroeconomic factors on individual-level preferences risks errors in the absence of suitable (individual-level) indicators of economic evaluations.[11] The latter are, we emphasize again, central to contemporary formulations of the economic approach (see Lewis-Beck and Stegmaier 2000).

Survey Data for the United States, Sweden, Norway, and the Netherlands

The data analyzed in this chapter are drawn from country-specific surveys. From a methodological standpoint, it would be ideal to analyze data drawn from cross-national surveys whose instrumentation reflects a fuller standardization of items across surveys. However, existing cross-national opinion surveys have not fielded the necessary items with which to analyze economic factors (i.e., items asking respondents their evaluation of their personal situation or that of the economy as a whole). This applies to the International Social Survey Program data that we analyze elsewhere in this book, and it is also true of archived data from the Political Action, World Values, and Eurobarometer surveys.

As a result, we must turn to country-specific surveys with a suitable array of items with which to measure economic evaluations, social factors, and mass policy preferences. This means, of course, that comparative results must be regarded with some degree of caution. For instance, cross-national differences might be influenced by variability in question-wording between the surveys. However, if a consistent pattern of results emerges across countries, it is less likely to be a methodological artifact. The degree of consistency we find in our results across countries lends, as we will see, some confidence to subsequent inferences.

The survey data we analyze are for the United States (a liberal democracy), Sweden and Norway (two social democratic countries), and the Netherlands (a Christian democracy). These data are all from repeated surveys of policy attitudes and political behavior, and our analyses are restricted to items that employ identical question-wording and response formats for surveys fielded within a specific country. The U.S. data are drawn from two sets of surveys: the *American National Election Studies* (Center for Political Studies 2003); and the *General Social Surveys* (Davis, Smith, and Marsden 2000). The Swedish data are from the *Swedish Election Studies* (Swedish Social Science Data Service 2002), and the Norwegian data are from the *Norwegian National Election Studies* (Statistics Norway 2003). Data for the Netherlands are from the *Dutch Election Studies* (Anker and Oppenhuis 1994, 1997; Aarts, van der Kolk, and Kamp 1999).

Measures

Table 5.1 summarizes the variables employed in the analysis of each country; in the chapter's appendix we provide a more detailed summary of how each of these variables is measured. The independent variables include, in most cases, measures of respondents' evaluations of the national economy ("sociotropic" evaluations), evaluations of their own economic circumstances ("egocentric" evaluations), and a range of social-cleavage and institutional variables. Variation in the availability of suitable policy preference measures across the four countries requires us to look at different preference measures. These include in all cases items relating to social provision, governmental responsibility, and social inequality.

TABLE 5.1   **Summary of Variables Used in Analysis of Policy Preferences**

	United States[a]	Sweden[b]	Norway[c]	Netherlands[d]
Independent variables				
	Sociotropic evaluations	Sociotropic evaluations	Sociotropic evaluations	Sociotropic evaluations
	Egocentric evaluations	Egocentric evaluations	Egocentric evaluations	Egocentric evaluations
	Class	Class		Class
	Religion	Union member		Religion
	Church attendance	Church attendance		Church attendance
	Race	Marital status		Gender
	Gender	Education		Marital status
	South			Education
	Marital status			Generation
	Education			
	Generation			
Dependent variables				
	Welfare spending	Public sector	Welfare state benefits	Income inequality
	Income inequality	Child care provision	Income inequality	Government porvision for jobs
	Welfare state benefits	Health insurance	Social services	Welfare state benefits
	Social services	Business regulation	Waste in taxes	
	Health care	Welfare state benefits	Business regulation	
	Racial equality	Market economy	Tax on high incomes	

[a]Data source: American National Election Studies and General Social Surveys.
[b]Data source: Swedish Election Studies 1956–99.
[c]Data source: Norwegian National Election Studies 1973–97.
[d]Data source: Dutch Parliamentary Election Study, 1989; Dutch Parliamentary Election Study, 1994; Dutch Parliamentary Election Study, 1998; Religion I; Religion II.

The Structure of Trends in Welfare State Preferences

Can patterns of change over time in preferences concerning the welfare state be captured by the expectations of the economic model? We begin our investigation of this question by presenting in figure 5.1 data for the United States, where sample means for each of the six items are presented.[12] The first item provides evidence of a net increase in aggregate preferences for public health care provision between the 1970s and late 1990s. This increase represents approximately a six-percentage-point shift in the direction of greater health effort. The next three items (for social service provision, welfare spending, and welfare state benefits) reveal greater over-time variability, but little net change. The last pair of items for attitudes toward racial equality and government reduction of income inequal-

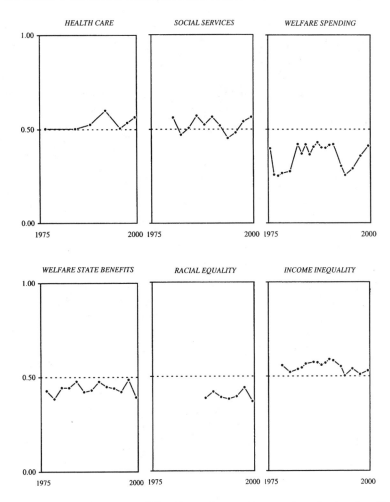

FIGURE 5.1. Trends in aggregate U.S. policy preferences. Data are from the American National Election Studies and the General Social Surveys (items have been recoded to a 0–1 range, where higher scores indicate greater support for welfare state-related policies).

ity are characterized, respectively, by modest (two- and three-percentage-point) net declines in support for government intervention.

While there has clearly been a degree of variation in U.S. policy preferences during the past several decades, the trends suggest little evidence of a cyclical pattern of change. Year-to-year variation is well under 10 percent of their standard deviations in four of the six items, while year-to-year variation for the other two items is 10 and 11 percent of their respective standard deviations. To put these findings into further perspective, variation in Americans' policy preferences during a given year is typically ten times more extensive than year-to-year variation in their aggregate preferences.

Turning next to the data for Sweden, the six panels in figure 5.2 present sample averages for policy preference items from the Swedish Election Studies data. The first five items all suggest a small net increase in pol-

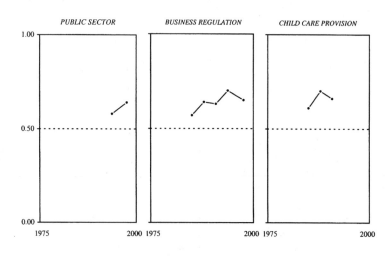

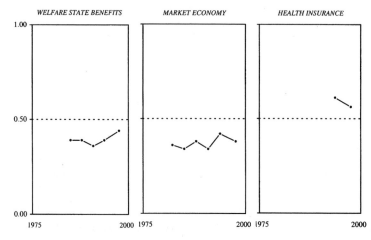

FIGURE 5.2. Trends in aggregate Swedish policy preferences. Data are from the Swedish Election Studies (items have been recoded to a 0–1 range, where higher scores indicate greater support for welfare state-related policies).

icy preferences for welfare state provisions. The sixth item reveals a four-percentage-point *decline* in aggregate preference for public health insurance (it should be noted that this inference is based on only two data points). Because the Swedish Election surveys are fielded less regularly than their American counterparts, the Swedish data series are thus typically shorter. With these caveats in mind, the Swedish data provide little evidence for a pattern of extensive year-to-year variability. Further, policy attitudes have tended to move monotonically in the direction of stronger welfare state support.

The third set of survey items comes from Norway. These present a comparable portrait of over-time change in aggregate policy preferences. Five of the six items in figure 5.3 show varying degrees of movement toward greater public preferences for welfare provisions, with the sixth item suggesting a net reduction in the level of aggregate preference for social service spending.

The fourth and final set of survey items is from the Dutch component of the International Social Survey Program and the Dutch Parliamentary Election Studies. In figure 5.4, the first item reveals a modest drop from 1981 to 1986 in public support for reducing income inequality, with no further change in aggregate opinion between 1986 and 1989. While the income inequality item ends in the 1980s, the two other items span the decade of the 1990s, and they both suggest increases in the level of Dutch preferences for government provision of jobs and welfare state benefits. None of these patterns of change is by itself indicative of a cyclical pattern of change. Some caution should of course be exercised in light of the short length or sparseness that characterizes these items.

Where do these results leave the economic and embedded preferences approaches? The economic model's expectation of temporal volatility is not supported by these data. In the majority of cases, aggregate trends in opinion show inertia or monotonic trends. Welfare state preferences among the four national publics have changed. Yet they have often moved steadily and without cyclicality.

Can Economic Factors Explain Aggregate Change in Welfare State Preferences?

We now turn to our second question regarding whether economic evaluations can account for trends in aggregate preferences. To get at this

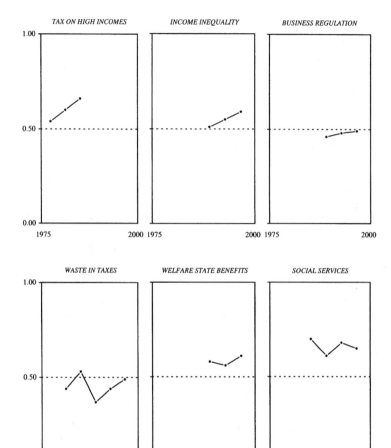

FIGURE 5.3. Trends in aggregate Norwegian policy preferences. Data are from the Norwegian Election Studies (items have been recoded to a 0–1 range, where higher scores indicate greater support for welfare state-related policies).

question, we analyze welfare state preference items from each of the four countries, using statistical models that measure the respective impacts of economic evaluations as well as several social factors. We then compare the initial predicted values with a second set of predictions that assume no change in the covariates measuring economic evaluations. If economic evaluations contribute to change in policy preferences, the two sets of estimates should diverge substantially. In particular, the second set of esti-

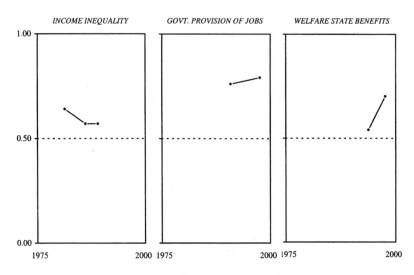

FIGURE 5.4. Trends in aggregate Dutch policy preferences. Data are from the International Social Survey Program and Dutch Parliamentary Election Studies (items have been recoded to a 0–1 range, where higher scores indicate greater support for welfare state-related policies).

mates based on assuming *no* change in economic variables should flatten out considerably. This would indicate that over-time patterns of aggregate change in welfare state preferences vanish in the absence of the stimulus provided by economic change.

We summarize the key predictions of our statistical analyses using a series of figures.[13] We begin with results for the United States in figure 5.5. The estimates connected by the *solid* lines show the predicted level of policy preferences for welfare state benefits. Estimates connected by *dotted* lines show the second predictions that are derived by assuming *no* change in both sociotropic and egocentric economic evaluations.[14]

These results do not provide support for the economic model's predictions. Rather than diverging substantially, both sets of estimates are quite similar. Moreover, instead of smoothing the pattern of aggregate change, estimates derived by assuming *no* economic change lead in some instances to slightly *larger* estimates of year-to-year change in policy preferences. This suggests that changes in the distribution of economic evaluations do not, by themselves, appear capable of accounting for aggregate change in American policy preferences.

Swedish results are displayed in figure 5.6. In comparison to the United States, the assumption of perfect stability in economic evaluations leads to

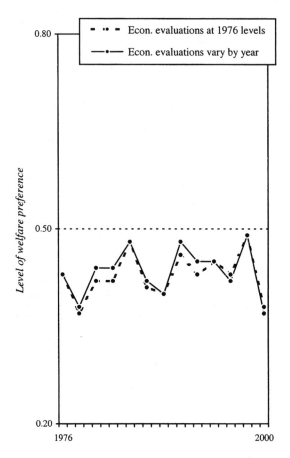

FIGURE 5.5. Effects of economic evaluations on aggregate policy preferences in the U.S.—
welfare state benefits. Data are from the American National Election Studies.

somewhat more divergent predictions of over-time change in Swedish policy preferences; this can be observed in the typically greater distance between estimates connected by solid versus dotted lines. Most importantly,
the pattern of change in question is still notably distant from the flat line
implied by the economic model. Further, holding constant the distribution
of economic evaluations leads in some cases to less year-to-year change in
aggregate policy preferences, and in others to greater year-to-year change.
Our thematic finding is that the Swedish results provide little support for
this expectation of the economic approach.

The Norwegian results presented in figure 5.7 show that changing levels

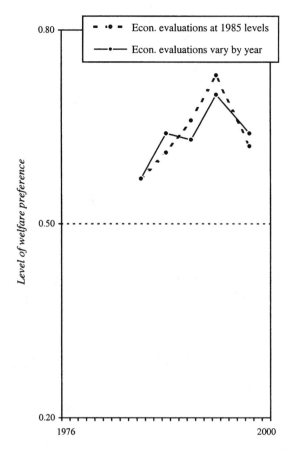

FIGURE 5.6. Effects of economic evaluations on aggregate policy preferences in Sweden—business regulation. Data are from the Swedish Election Studies.

of economic evaluations have no appreciable impact on trends in policy preferences. The near-congruence of the two sets of estimates in the figure shows that aggregate change in economic evaluations matters even less than in the cases of Sweden and the United States. Trends in aggregate policy preferences in Norway are largely independent of aggregate change in citizens' economic evaluations.

Results for the Netherlands are presented in figure 5.8. Recall that there are only three Dutch policy preferences in the trend analyses, and only one of these was fielded in surveys that contain economic evaluation items with which to develop a multivariate analysis. Notwithstanding

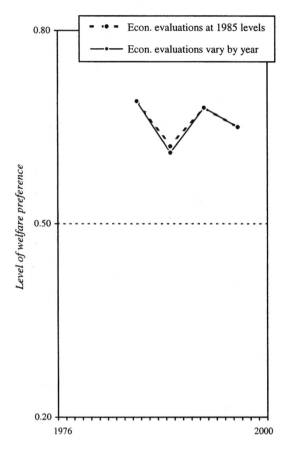

FIGURE 5.7. Effects of economic evaluations on aggregate policy preferences in Norway—social services. Data are from the Norwegian Election Studies.

these caveats, results of our analysis show that instead of flattening out the pattern of aggregate change in Dutch policy preferences, holding constant the level of economic evaluations results in a *larger* shift in aggregate preferences. This result is inconsistent with expectations of the economic approach to understanding policy preferences.

Social Versus Economic Sources of Welfare State Preferences

A third and final point of difference between economic and embedded preferences models concerns the relative magnitude of economic factors

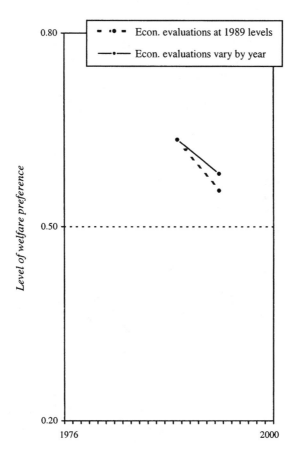

FIGURE 5.8. Effects of economic evaluations on aggregate policy preferences in the Netherlands—inequality. Data are from the Dutch Election Studies.

as sources of *individuals'* welfare state preferences. We evaluate the expectation that economic evaluations will be a major, perhaps dominant, mechanism behind the acquisition of these preferences, particularly in comparison to social factors. For these analyses, we compare the predicted effects
of economic evaluations versus social factors on policy preference items.[15]

We start with results for the United States, displayed in figure 5.9. In the
left-hand panel of the figure, we compare the magnitude of racial and class
cleavages with the corresponding magnitude of economic (sociotropic and
egocentric) evaluations. The racial cleavage has by far the largest impact
on policy preferences, followed at a distance by sociotropic evaluations,
egocentric evaluations, and then the class cleavage.

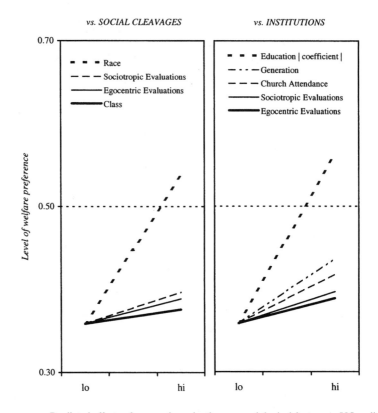

FIGURE 5.9. Predicted effects of economic evaluations vs. sociological factors on U.S. policy preferences. Data are from the American National Election Studies.

In the right-hand panel, we compare the magnitude of institutional factors relating to education, church attendance, and generational differences with sociotropic and egocentric evaluations. The effects of education[16] are even larger than the earlier effects of race, and they dwarf the effects of economic factors. The next largest factor is generational differences, with the most recent birth cohort being considerably more supportive of public social provision than the reference generation. Church attendance also has greater effects on policy preferences than either sociotropic or egocentric evaluations.

Parallel results for Sweden are presented in figure 5.10. Starting with the comparison between social cleavages and economic evaluations, the class cleavage has the largest effect, followed by sociotropic evaluations,[17] union membership, and egocentric evaluations. Egocentric evaluations, it

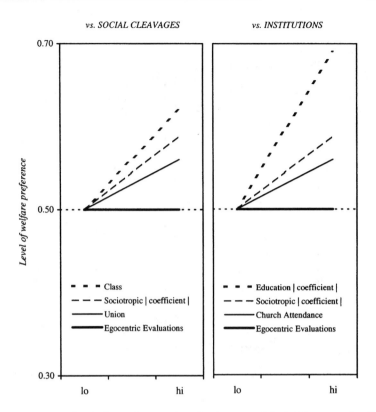

FIGURE 5.10. Predicted effects of economic evaluations vs. sociological factors on Swedish policy preferences. Data are from the Swedish Election Studies.

should be noted, represent a non-effect, as indicated by the absence of any change in predicted values across levels of this covariate.

Looking at institutional factors in Sweden, the predicted effects of education are quite large, followed again by sociotropic evaluations, church attendance, and finally egocentric evaluations. Similar to the U.S. results, sociotropic evaluations clearly exert a nontrivial influence over the formation of policy preferences in Sweden. Nevertheless, a variety of social-cleavage and institutional factors also have significant effects. Notably, the causal influence of sociotropic (and also egocentric) evaluations is smaller in comparison to both the class cleavage and educational institutions in Sweden.

Results for the Netherlands are presented in figure 5.11. Sociotropic evaluations have the single largest effect of any independent variable

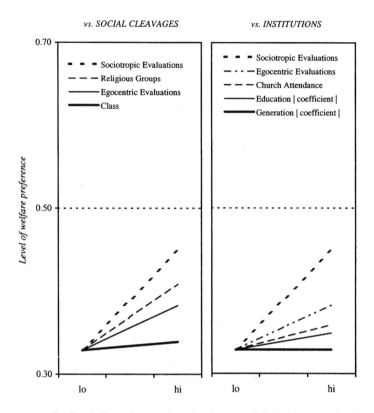

FIGURE 5.11. Predicted effects of economic evaluations vs. sociological factors on Dutch policy preferences. Data are from the Dutch National Election Studies.

in the analysis, followed by the influence of religious group differences. Whereas class and generational differences represent trivial effects, the influence of egocentric evaluations is more substantial in Holland. For its part, church attendance exerts a modest influence on attitudes, where that effect is smaller than that of both types of economic evaluations and the influence of religious group memberships.

The thematic finding that emerges from these results is that economic evaluations are far from being a dominant factor in the formation of individuals' preferences. Instead, numerous cleavage and institutional factors operate in the acquisition of policy preferences. Moreover, the influence of economic evaluations is eclipsed by the larger effects of specific social factors within two of the polities we have analyzed. Macroeconomic shifts experienced by individuals clearly influence their subsequent policy preferences, expressed through the operation of economic evaluations. But they do so amidst the operation of a variety of other causal factors. By itself, the economic approach would provide an incomplete account of the processes shaping the acquisition and maintenance of social policy preferences among individuals.

Microfoundations of Opinion/Social Policy Linkages

Once we acknowledge the sizable influence of mass policy preferences over government output—the argument of the first four chapters of this book—a central question concerns the causal origins of these preferences. In this chapter, we have contrasted economic and embedded preferences approaches to better understand how to account for the development of citizens' attitudes toward the welfare state. We considered three specific challenges: (1) whether aggregate trends in policy preferences follow the cyclical pattern suggested by the economic model; (2) whether economic evaluations are sufficient to explain patterns of aggregate change in policy preferences; and finally, (3) whether economic evaluations overwhelm other factors in accounting for individuals' policy preferences.

Our results, drawing upon new analyses of survey data from four countries, in each case favor the inclusive embedded preferences approach to policy preferences over the economic approach.[18] Welfare state preferences, we contend, are influenced by individuals' locations within social structures and institutions, and also by their collective memories concerning welfare state development. To be sure, the magnitude of these factors will vary across countries and over time. The key thematic point is that factors of this sort change slowly over short periods of time, contributing to inertial tendencies in aggregate opinion.

We conclude by reiterating the relevance of inertia and social embeddedness in understanding the evolution of public attitudes toward social provision. Both themes are readily apparent in classic studies of mass opinion, and they have been further developed in Page and Shapiro's (1992) comprehensive analysis of trends in U.S. opinion. In this chapter, we have suggested that these insights can be extended with cross-national evidence. We think the evidence is compelling that whatever the level of support for social provision, those attitudes are deeply rooted and tend to move slowly over time.

Appendix: Measures Used in the Analysis

In this chapter, we draw upon data from national surveys fielded in four countries: the United States, Sweden, Norway, and the Netherlands. We use six separate policy preference items for our analysis of the U.S. data. These items ask respondents their degree of preference for government versus private/market-based policies with respect to welfare spending, income inequality, benefits, social services, health care, and racial equality. As noted in table 5.2, the welfare spending and income inequality items are from the *General Social Surveys,* while the remaining four items are from the *National Election Studies.*

We list in table 5.3 independent variables in our analysis of the U.S. data. Our measurement of economic evaluations closely follows contemporary work on the economic model of policy preferences (e.g., Kiewiet 1983; see also Erikson et al. 2002a). Most analysts view sociotropic evaluations as having greater effects than egocentric evaluations, and we include measures of both in the analyses.

With respect to social cleavage factors in the U.S., our independent variables are for the class cleavage, race, gender, and region. We use six dummy variables to measure the class cleavage, following recent political-sociological work on class (Manza and Brooks 1999). Three additional dummy variables respectively measure racial, gender, and region-based cleavages. Regarding institutional factors, our analyses include independent variables for the major institutions of religion, family, education, and generation. Following contemporary work on the U.S. religion cleavage (e.g., Smith 1998; Steensland et al. 2000), six dummy variables for religion distinguish among evangelical, mainline, and black Protestants, and, further, among Catholic and Jewish respondents and members of other religious traditions (with the reference category being for nonreligious individuals). A measure of church attendance captures the level of individuals' religious participation. Exposure to family institutions is measured using a dummy variable for marital status, and experience with educational institutions is measured using a continuous variable for the highest year of respondents' education. With respect to generational differences in attitudes, we include in the analysis a pair of dummy variables to identify three birth cohorts: individuals born before 1940, those born between 1940 and 1959, and those born after 1959. Our statistical models for the United States (and the other three countries) include dummy variables to take into account the effects of time period.

TABLE 5.2 **Dependent Variables in the Analysis of U.S. Policy Preferences**

Variables	Question Wording (Coding)
Welfare spending	*We are faced with many problems in this country, none of which can be solved easily or inexpensively. I am going to name some of these problems, and for each one I'd like you to tell me whether you think we're spending too much money on it, too little money, or about the right amount: Welfare.* (1. too much; 2. about the right amount; 3. too little).
Income inequality	*Some people think that the government in Washington ought to reduce the income differences between the rich and the poor, perhaps by raising the taxes of wealthy families or by giving income assistance to the poor. Others think that the government should not concern itself with reducing this income difference between the rich and the poor. Here is a card with a scale from 1 to 7.* (1. government should not concern itself with reducing income differences 7. government ought to reduce income differences)
Welfare state benefits	*Some people feel the government in Washington should see to it that every person has a job and a good standard of living. Others think the government shuld just let each person ge ahead on their own. Where would you place yourself on this scale, or haven't you thought much about this?* (1. government let each person get ahead 7. government see to job and good standard of living)
Social services	*Some people think the government should provide fewer services, even in areas such as health and education in order to reduce spending. Other people feel it is important for the government to provide many more services even if it means an increase in spending. Where would you place yourself on this scale, or haven't you thought much about this?* (1. fewer services, reduce spending 7. more services, increase spending)
Health care	*There is much concern about the rapid rise in medical and hospital costs. Some people feel there should be a government insurance plan which would cover all medical and hospital expenses for everyone. Others feel that all medical expenses should be paid by individuals, and through private insurance plans like Blue Cross or other company paid plans. Where would you place yourself on this scale, or haven't you thought much about this?* (1. private insurance plan 7. government insurance plan)
Racial equality	*Some people feel that the government in Washington should make every effort to improve the social and economic position of blacks. Others feel that the government should not make any special effort to help blacks because they should help themselves. Where would you place yourself on this scale, or haven't you thought much about this?* (1. blacks should help themselves 7. government should help blacks)

Note: Data are from the American National Election Studies, with exception of the first two variables (these are from the General Social Surveys).

Variables in the analysis for Sweden are listed in table 5.4. Six policy preference items ask respondents their degree of preference for government versus private/market-based policies with respect to public sector cuts, child-care provision, health insurance, business regulation, welfare state benefits, and market economy initiatives. The next two items measure

TABLE 5.3 **Independent Variables in the Analysis of U.S. Policy Preferences**

Variables	Question Wording (Coding)
Sociotropic evaluations	*How about the economy. Would you say that over the past year the nation's economy has gotten better, stayed about the same, or gotten worse?* (1. better; 2. same; 3. worse)
Egocentric evaluations	*We are interested in how people are getting along financially these days. Would you say that you (and your family living here) are better off or worse off financially than you were a year ago?* (1. better; 2. same; 3. worse)
Class	6 dummy variables for: professionals, managers, routine white-collar, self-employed, skilled workers, non-skilled workers, (non-labor force = reference)
Religion	6 dummy variables for: evangelical Protestant, mainline Protestant, black Protestant, Catholic, Jewish, other religion (no religion = reference)
Church attendance	1. attend every week; 2. attend almost every week; 3. attend once or twice a month; 4. attend a few times a year; 5. attend never
Race	African-American = 1 (else = reference)
Gender	Female = 1 (male = reference)
South	Southern residence = 1 (else = reference)
Marital status	unmarried/divorced/widowed = 1 (married = reference)
Education	highest year attained
Generation	2 dummy variables for: born 1940–59; > 1960 (born < 1940 = reference)

Note: Data are from the American National Election Studies.

sociotropic and egocentric evaluations. Regarding social cleavage factors, we include in the analysis four dummy variables with which to measure a simplified version of the class typology used for the U.S. data. We also include a dummy variable for union membership, given the historical importance of labor unions as a further source of class-related mobilization and identity in Sweden. Institutional factors are church attendance (measured as level of self-reported attendance), marital status (measured as a dummy variable), and education (measured in years). Note that in light of religious homogeneity in Sweden, we do not attempt to analyze Swedish religious institutions in terms of denominational memberships, focusing instead on attendance level as the key process through which religious influence is transmitted.

Table 5.5 lists the variables used in the analysis of the Norwegian data. Six policy preference items ask respondents their degree of preference for government versus private/market-based policies with respect to welfare state benefits, income inequality, social services, the extent of waste in taxes, business regulation, and tax cuts for individuals with high incomes.

TABLE 5.4 **Variables in the Analysis of Swedish Policy Preferences**

Variables	Question Wording (Coding)
Dependent variables	
Public sector	*I will now read to a list of policies which some people think ought to be implemented in Sweeden. Using one of the answers on this card, what is your opinion about the following proposal: Reduce the size of the public sector.* (1. very good proposal; 2. fairly good proposal; 3. neither good nor bad proposal; 4. fairly bad proposal; 5. very bad proposal)
Child care provision	*Using one of the answers on this card, what is your opinion about the proposal to build more day care centers for children?* (1. very good proposal; 2. fairly good proposal; 3. neither good nor bad proposal; 4. fairly bad proposal; 5. very bad proposal)
Health insurance	*Increase the proportion of medical care run by private interests.* (1. very good proposal; 2. fairly good proposal; 3. neither good nor bad proposal; 4. fairly bad proposal; 5. very bad proposal)
Business regulation	*Leading bankers and industry people will get far too influential unless society is given the chance to control private business and industry.* (1. disagree completely; 2. disagree on the whole; 3. agree on the whole; 4. agree completely)
Welfare state benefits	*Social reforms in this country have gone so far that the state should reduce rather than increase social benefits and support for people.* (1. disagree completely; 2. disagree on the whole; 3. agree on the whole; 4. agree completely)
Market economy	*On this card I have a list of suggestions of different kinds of societies which some people think we should work toward in the future in Sweden. I would like to hear what you think of the suggestions. What do think of the suggestion to: Work towards a society with more private enterprise and a more market-oriented economy.* (0 = very good suggestion 5 = neither good nor bad suggestion . . . 10 = very bad suggestion)
Independent variables	
Sociotropic evaluations	*How has, in your opinion, the Swedish economy changed during the last 2–3 years?* (1.improved; 2. remained the same; 3. gotten worse)
Egocentric evaluations	*If you compare your own economic situation to what it was 2–3 years ago, has it improved, remained the same or gotten worse?* (1. improved; 2. remained the same; 3. gotten worse)
Class	4 dummy variables for: self-employed, managers, all white-collar employees, workers (non-labor force = reference)
Union member	member = 1 (else = reference)
Church attendance	1. at least once a month; 2. a few times a year; 3. less often; 4. never
Marital status	unmarried/divorced/widowed = 1 (married = reference)

Note: Data are from the *Swedish Election Studies.*

TABLE 5.5   **Variables in the Analysis of Norwegian Policy Preferences**

Variables	Question Wording (Coding)
Dependent variables	
Welfare state benefits	*Now for the subject of social security, welfare, etc. Many people believe that we in Norway have acquired more than enough in the way of social security and welfare benefits over the years, and that we should seek to limit them in the future; while others maintain that we should keep our present system and if necessary develop it further. Do you think that in the future we ought to have less social security and welfare benefits, that we should retain them as they are at present, or do you think the system should be further developed?* (1. should be less benefits. 2. should be maintained at present level; 3. should be developed further)
Income inequality	*We have some further statements. We use the same answer alternatives as before. Do you react with complete agreement, qualified disagreement, or complete disagreement to the following statements? To exhort people to greater effort, we should be willing to accept bigger differences in wage levels.* (1. complete agreement; 2. qualified agreement; 3. yes and no; 4. qualified disagreement; 5. complete disagreement)
Social services	*It is more important to develop public services than to reduce taxation.* (1. complete agreement; 2. qualified agreement; 3. yes and no; 4. qualified disagreement; 5. complete disagreement)
Waste in taxes	*Do you think that those who govern waste a large part of the money we pay in taxes, that they waste some of it, or that they waste very little of this money?* (1. largepart; 2. some; 3. very little)
Business regulation	*I shall now again read to you a few proposals. . . . We should reduce government control over private industry.* (1. complete agreement; 2. qualified agreement; 3. yes and no; 4. qualified disagreement; 5. complete disagreement)
Tax on high incomes	*Cut tax on high income.* (1. complete agreement; 2. qualified agreement; 3. yes and no; 4. qualified disagreement; 5. complete disagreement)
Independent variables	
Sociotropic evaluations	*Would you say that the country's economy during the past year has improved, has remained on the same level, or is in worse shape than previously?* (1. improved; 2. remained the same level; 3. worse)
Egocentric evaluations	*We are interested in knowing something about people's current financial situation. Would you say that your financial situation and that of your household is better or worse than it was a year ago?* (1. better than now; 2. same; 3. worse)

Note: Data are from the *Norwegian Election Studies.*

The next two items measure sociotropic and egocentric evaluations. Note that because data on social cleavages and institutions within the Norwegian surveys are considerably more sparse (or less comparable), our multivariate analyses are restricted to the variables for economic evaluations. Table 5.6 summarizes the variables in our analysis of the Netherlands.

TABLE 5.6 **Variables in the Analysis of Dutch Policy Preferences**

Variables	Question Wording (Coding)
Dependent variables	
Income inequality	*Some people think that the differences in incomes in our country should be increased. Others think that these differences should be decreased. Of course, there are also people whose opinion is somewhere in between. And where woul you place yourself on this line?* (1. larger differences . . . 7. smaller differences)
Government porvision for jobs	*On the whole, do you think it should be or should not be the government's responsibility to: Provide a job for everyone who wants one?* (1. definitely should not be; 2. probably should not be; 3. probably should be; 4. definitely should be)
Welfare state benefits	*On the whole, do you think it should be or should not be the government's responsibility to: Reduce income differences between the rich and poor?* (1. definitely should not be; 2. probably should not be; 3. probably should be; 4. definitely should be)
Independent variables	
Sociotropic evaluations	*I would like to ask a few questions about what you think of the policies that the government has conducted during the past four years. First, the general economic situation: do you think that the economic situation has been influenced favorably, unfavorably, or neither by the past government policies?* (1. favorable; 2. neither; 3. unfavorable)
Egocentric evaluations	*And your personal financial situation: do you think that your personal financial situation has been influenced favorably, unfavorably, or neither by the past government policies?* (1. favorable; 2. neither; 3. unfavorable)
Class	4 dummy variables for: self-employed, managers, salaried employees, workers (non-labor force = reference)
Union member	member = 1 (else = reference)
Religious groups	3 dummy variables for: no religion, Catholic, other religion (Protestant = reference)
Church attendance	1. at least once a week; 2. 2 or 3 times a month; 3. once a month; 4. several times a year; 5. (almost) never
Gender	Female = 1 (male = reference)
Marital status	unmarried/divorced/widowed = 1 (married = reference)
Education	Highest year attained
Generation	2 dummy variables for: born 1940–59; > 1960 (born < 1940 = reference)

Note: Data are from the Dutch Election Studies, with the exception of Government provision of jobs and Welfare state benefits items (these are from the International Social Survey Program).

In comparison to the preceding data, the Dutch surveys contain fewer suitable policy preference items, and our analyses thus focus on three items concerning attitudes toward income inequality, government provision of jobs, and welfare state benefits. Regarding independent variables, dummy variables for class, union membership, and gender measure social cleavage factors. We measure institutional factors relating to religion using a variable for church attendance level, and three dummy variables for Protestants, Catholics, and members of other religious traditions (with nonreligious respondents as the reference category). A dummy variable for marital status and a continuous variable for education measure individuals' exposure to the institutions of family and school. With respect to generational differences in attitudes, we include in the analysis a pair of dummy variables to identify three birth cohorts: individuals born before 1940, those born between 1940 and 1959, and those born after 1959.

CHAPTER SIX

The Patterning of Social Policy Responsiveness

The analyses we have presented to this point in the book have focused primarily on trends and cross-national differences in overall welfare spending relative to a country's gross domestic product. Such a focus is appropriate, because research has demonstrated that overall social spending effort powerfully captures the influence of welfare states on the pattern of stratification and inequality. Domain-specific measures, by contrast, can present a limited, even at times misleading, portrait of trends and cross-national differences in welfare states. As we saw in chapter 3, this problem can be acute when spending or entitlement measures are limited exclusively to cash benefits, thereby neglecting the service dimensions of contemporary welfare states. Nonetheless, consideration of domain-specific policies, alongside analysis of aggregated welfare output, can provide additional valuable insights about the patterning of responsiveness.

We thus turn in this chapter to consider in more detail one such issue: the magnitude of opinion/policy linkages across aggregated versus domain-specific dimensions of social policy output. Are the effects of policy preferences larger or smaller for specific policy domains in comparison to the aggregated output of welfare states? We might anticipate that the effects of both officials' strategic activities and organized interest groups are *larger* with respect to specific policy domains. This would mean that the policy effects of mass preferences are muted or even displaced in the face of interest group influence and the autonomy of politicians. Opinion/policy linkage would thus be stronger with respect to aggregated welfare output. Certainly, we expect to find some differences in linkages when we look across policy domains.

In this chapter we analyze the magnitude of opinion/policy linkages across aggregated versus specific social policy domains. Complementing our earlier multivariate analysis of aggregated welfare output, we consider six further measures of spending or entitlements within specific policy domains, such as sickness benefits and expenditures on the aged. As a prelude to our analyses, we begin by outlining two different conceptions of what we mean by "policy responsiveness."

Two Types of Policy Responsiveness

Global Policy Responsiveness

The simplest expectation concerning the interrelationship of mass opinion and social policy is that this linkage operates *globally,* across multiple policy domains. Government officials incorporate information about voter preferences by organizing the overall output and contours of social policy in accord with these preferences. Rather than seeking to tailor (all) specific policy domains in perfect accordance with mass preferences, it is in the aggregate shape of policy output that officials respond most consistently to public opinion.

Global policy responsiveness is the expectation of a body of recent, U.S.-centered research on opinion/policy linkages (Stimson et al. 1995; Erikson et al. 2002a, 2002b; see also Burstein 1998; Manza and Cook 2002). Global policy responsiveness represents a "simple" model, because it is eminently compatible with limited or low information on the part of both citizens and elected officials. With respect to citizens, global policy responsiveness implies that members of the public care about, and attend primarily to, the overall level of welfare spending or provision, but not necessarily to the details pf any particular program. A more demanding set of assumptions would be that citizens also assess the output of government within specific domains. This would mean that citizens are capable of processing information on the policy-specific activities of government.

Turning to government officials, global policy responsiveness implies that their information and incentives concerning mass opinion apply primarily to voters' social policy preferences in the aggregate, that is, the degree to which welfare provisions are extensive versus minimal, generous versus stingy. As before, this represents a low/limited-information model in comparison to the further assumption that politicians incorporate voter preferences in developing policies within specific domains such as unemployment insurance or family policy. Here, politicians need to know only the general outlines of mass preferences to respond effectively.

Global policy responsiveness implies that opinion/policy linkages will be stronger with respect to aggregate government output than to domain-specific policies. This is because, by hypothesis, politicians will tend to have greater information and incentive to respond to mass opinion through the overall amount or direction of welfare policy while retaining autonomy at the level of concrete policies. In considering the global responsiveness thesis, we look primarily at the contrast between aggregate and domain-specific opinion/policy linkages. As before, evidence that the magnitude of domain-specific linkages rivals (or is larger than) the linkage with aggregated output would be inconsistent with the global responsiveness hypothesis.

Domain-Specific Policy Responsiveness

Limited information or selective attentiveness on the part of voters and policymakers will tend to result in social policy responsiveness occurring primarily with respect to the overall output of welfare states. But a "higher-quality" pattern of responsiveness (Wlezien 2004) is also possible. This occurs when politicians respond to mass policy preferences by tailoring the output of government policy within specific domains to what they think the public wants. One way this could happen is by politicians incorporating information about voters' *domain-specific* preferences (Soroka and Wlezien 2005), where these preferences are assumed to vary with the policy domain in question. Family policy, for instance, could be formed through officials gauging citizens' specific preferences concerning child care or parental leave rather than their more general views of social welfare provision.

A second way that domain-specific responsiveness occurs is when politicians incorporate (the same) information about voters' preferences but in ways that *vary* across domain. For example, health spending may increase in response to public attitudes toward health provision, or health spending may increase more than unemployment insurance in response to pressures from the public for better social services and supports as a whole. In this way, politicians may strategically incorporate the (same) signal in different ways across policy domains.

For the purposes of this chapter, our main interest is with the possibility that patterns of domain-specific responsiveness differ in magnitude from the linkage between preferences and aggregate welfare output. As discussed earlier, it is this scenario that distinguishes the global responsiveness expectation from alternative patterns in which opinion/policy linkages are larger within specific policy domains. But we also consider the comparative magnitudes of domain-specific opinion/policy linkages. As discussed in greater detail below, these comparisons are informative with respect to the likelihood of interest group influence and politicians' degree of strategic discretion.

Data and Measures

Dependent Variables

In this chapter, we analyze opinion/policy linkages within seven policy domains. For purposes of comparison, we draw from the earlier analysis in chapters 2 and 3, of the influence of mass policy preferences over aggregate welfare output. In particular, estimates of the influence of mass policy preferences for our primary measure of overall welfare effort provide a baseline for evaluating the magnitude of further linkages involving policy-specific domains. As before, overall welfare effort is our primary measure of the aggregated output of welfare states.

As an initial point of comparison, we also make use of Scruggs's (2004) recently released index of benefits generosity. This index summarizes government-provided replacement income across the three core domains of pensions, unemployment, and sickness benefits. It is summarized, alongside the measure of overall welfare state effort, in table 6.1.

The remaining measures in table 6.1 are for policy-specific domains. We deliberately consider a diverse array of such domains, including those relating to government-provided replacement income, and those with a large service-oriented component. Our first three domains are for sickness, unemployment, and pension benefits for single persons. These replacement income data are extracted from the *Welfare State Entitlements* dataset. The next dependent variable is for per capita public health spending (OECD 2005). This variable measures per capita government expenditures on health, where values are scaled to 2000 U.S. dollars using PPP ratios to maximize cross-national comparability. Our final domain-specific measure is for public sector employment. This measure is drawn from the *Comparative Welfare States Dataset* (Huber et al. 2004). Inclusion of this measure provides an additional focus on the domain-specific dimensions of service provision, for public sector employment is a defining (and variable) feature of contemporary welfare states (Huber and Stephens 2001: chap. 3).

TABLE 6.1 **Dependent Variables in the Analysis**

Variable	Description	Data Source
Overall welfare state effort[a]	Government expenditures on cash and in-kind benefits and services as a percentage of GDP	*Social Expenditures Database* (SOCX)
Benefits generosity[b]	Index of average income replacement for pensions, unemployment benefits, and sickness benefits.	*Welfare State Entitlements Dataset* (WSI)
Sickness benefits[b]	Ratio of net insurance benefit for general short-term illness to net income for single person earning the average production worker (APW) wage.	WSI
Unemployment benefits[b]	Ratio of net unemployment insurance benefit to net income for an unmarried single person earning the average production worker (APW) wage.	WSI
Pension benefits[b]	Ratio of net public pension paid to a person earning the APW wage in each year of their working career upon retirement.	WSI
Per capita public health spending[a]	Per capita public expenditures on health, purchasing power parity (PPP) adjusted to 2000 U.S. dollars.	SOCX
Public sector employment[c]	Civilian government employment as a percentage of the working age population, age 15–64.	*Comparative Welfare States Dataset* (CWS)

[a]Country-years in the analysis: Australia (1987, 1991, 1997, 1999), Austria (1994, 2000), Canada (1997), France (1998, 1999), Germany (1986, 1991, 1992, 1997, 1999), Ireland (1992, 1997, 1999), Italy (1986, 1991, 1997, 2000), Japan (1997, 1999), Netherlands (1992, 1999), New Zealand (1992, 1998, 1999), Norway (1991, 1997, 1999), Spain (1997, 1999), Sweden (1997, 1999), Switzerland (2000), the United Kingdom (1991, 1992, 1999), and the United States (1986, 1991, 1992, 1997, 1999).

[b]Country-years in the analysis: Australia (1987, 1991, 1997, 1999), Austria (1987, 1994, 2000), Canada (1997), France (1998, 1999), Germany (1986, 1991, 1992, 1997, 1999), Ireland (1992, 1997, 1999), Italy (1986, 1991, 1997, 2000), Japan (1997, 1999), Netherlands (1992, 1999), New Zealand (1992, 1998, 1999), Norway (1991, 1997, 1999), Sweden (1997, 1999), Switzerland (2000), the United Kingdom (1991, 1992, 1999), and the United States (1986, 1991, 1992, 1997, 1999).

[c]Country-years in the analysis: Australia (1987, 1991, 1997, 1999), Austria (1987, 1994), Canada (1997), France (1998, 1999), Germany (1986, 1991, 1992, 1997, 1999), Ireland (1992, 1997, 1999), Italy (1986, 1991, 1997), Japan (1997, 1999), Netherlands (1992), Norway (1991, 1997, 1999), Sweden (1997, 1999), the United Kingdom (1991, 1992, 1999), and the United States (1986, 1991, 1992, 1997, 1999).

Independent Variables and Standardized Coefficients

Our statistical approach and independent variables are the same as those employed in preceding chapters. As part of the analysis, we also evaluate evidence for interaction effects involving mass policy preferences for each dependent variable. We present coefficient estimates for the main effect of the policy preference covariates, and, where significant, coefficients for interaction effects.[1]

Ultimately, we want to compare the magnitude of coefficients reflecting the influence of policy preferences across different dependent variables. In this way, we can gauge the variation in magnitude of opinion/policy linkages across policy domains. To facilitate this comparison, we present standardized coefficients, where these take into account differences in the distribution of the dependent and independent variables.

Analyses of Opinion/Policy Linkages

In table 6.2, we summarize results of the analysis. The first column displays the coefficient for the linkage between policy preferences and our aggregated measure of welfare output: overall welfare spending effort. This provides a baseline for considering the benefits generosity index (in the second column) and the policy-specific measures in the remainder of the table. To facilitate comparison across dependent variables for different policy domains, we present standardized coefficients in the table.

Starting, then, with our measure of aggregated welfare output, the first column's main effect estimate indicates that a standard unit increase in policy preferences raises welfare state effort by .50 units.[2] At .23, the second column's estimate reveals a smaller, nonsignificant linkage between mass policy preferences and benefits generosity. In contrast, the coefficient for sickness benefits is significant, with a value of .38.

Of the next two coefficients, the estimate for unemployment benefits is not significant, but the estimate for pension benefits is both large and significant. Indeed, at .83, this opinion/policy linkage is even larger than the linkage to aggregate welfare output. But the negative sign of the interaction with liberal democracies qualifies this finding in an important way. Specifically, the −.66 coefficient means that the predicted effect of policy preferences on pension benefits within liberal democracies is only .17, suggesting a weak linkage in comparison to social and Christian democracies.

What of the final pair of policy domains? Per capita public health is characterized by a significant linkage to mass opinion, and one whose magnitude is half that of overall welfare effort. Results for public employment tell a different story: the coefficient in the first row is not significant, but the interaction between preferences and social democracies *is*. This provides evidence that like pension benefits, social policy responsiveness can vary quite dramatically across types of polities. In general, public employment responsiveness to mass opinion is weak, yet in social democracies it

TABLE 6.2 **Standardized Coefficients for Analyzing Social Policy Outputs across Domains**

Independent Variables	Overall welfare effort (N = 44)	Benefits generosity (N = 43)	Sickness benefits (N = 43)	Unemployment benefits (N = 43)	Pension benefits (N = 43)	Per capita public health (N = 44)	Public employment (N = 36)
Policy preferences	.50* (3.76)	.23 (1.11)	.38* (2.09)	.22 (1.05)	.83* (3.42)	.24* (3.13)	−.06 (−.27)
Policy prefs. × lib. democracy	—	—	—	—	−.66* (−2.20)	—	—
Policy prefs. × soc. democracy	—	—	—	—	—	—	.52* (2.50)

Notes: Coefficients estimated by OLS with robust-cluster standard errors; and asterisk next to a coefficient denotes significance at the .05 level; "—" indicates coefficient for interaction is not significant in initial tests.

is, instead, rather strong. A key message of these results is accordingly that responsiveness can be patterned in more complicated ways within specific domains of social policymaking in comparison to the aggregate output of welfare states.

Conclusion

How do opinion/policy linkages vary across social policy domains? Do government officials respond to citizens' preferences primarily through the overall level of welfare output, or instead by tailoring domain-specific policies? In this chapter, we have sought to provide a provisional answer to these questions, extending our earlier multivariate analyses to develop comparisons with opinion/policy linkages within specific domains.

Thematically, our results tend to support the global responsiveness thesis. The linkage between policy preferences and our measure of aggregate welfare output appears larger than policy responsiveness within specific domains. This holds in five of the six specific domains we have investigated, but two caveats are in order, relating to the domains of pension benefits and public employment.

In both these domains, a key source of complexity is the high level of responsiveness in some types of polities (European democracies for pension benefits, and social democracies for public employment) but not all polities. This cross-national patterning provides evidence for the importance that context can have for social policy responsiveness. These results call for further investigations, and the study of domain-specific policy responsiveness is in a promising stage of development (Wlezien 2004; Burstein 2006). With these caveats in mind, we conclude that there is a degree of support for the global responsiveness view when it comes to social policymaking. Government officials tend to respond most vigorously to mass policy preferences through the overall level of welfare provision.

Sources of Variation in Opinion/Social Policy Linkages

These methodological considerations and our results lead us to reflect upon a final issue: variability across policy domain in politicians' strategic discretion and the influence of interest groups. Processes of the latter sort are challenging to measure cross-nationally (cf. Knoke et al. 1996). They have, instead, been at the center of a rich and case-oriented literature on policy conflict and change within specific domains (e.g., Jacobs and Shapiro 2000; McAdam and Su 2002; Burstein 2003). We have not directly incorporated these processes into the analyses, but our results have some relevant implications.

We find a pattern of substantial differences in policy responsiveness across domains. This is much in line with the operation of interest-group influence and a degree of strategic discretion on the part of politicians. Instances of nonresponsiveness, in particular, are especially telling. They imply that the signal of mass opinion is overridden by other factors such as the activities of interest groups and the power of officials to strategically avoid incorporating citizen preferences into the policymaking process.

Clearly, these implications merit further study and scrutiny, and systematically attempting to distinguish interest-group influence from the discretionary power of politicians is an important challenge. But not to be lost amidst these reflections is our larger thematic finding concerning the dynamics of aggregate welfare policymaking. In comparison to variability in responsiveness within specific social policy domains, opinion/policy linkages appear strongest with respect to the overall size and output of welfare states.

CHAPTER SEVEN

Embedded Preferences and Welfare State Trajectories

What will the next wave of social, economic, and ideological developments in capitalist democracies mean for the future of welfare states? At the beginning of the twenty-first century, mature welfare states start from a substantial baseline of benefits and service provision. The sizable—yet cross-nationally variable—level of welfare state provision can be seen in recent levels of per capita expenditures.[1] Consider the social democracies of Scandinavia, where welfare state provisions and spending in the postwar era have set a standard for comprehensiveness and public generosity. Fully 29 percent of Swedish gross domestic product in 2001 was devoted to public social provision, amounting to $8,584 per capita worth of cash and in-kind benefits and services.

Scandinavian welfare states are, of course, distinctive in their approach to, and levels of, social provision. But trends toward higher levels of social spending effort elsewhere in Western Europe have led to greater similarity between social and Christian democracies. The average of 26 percent of GDP ($7,805 per capita) devoted to welfare state provisions in Christian democracies is very similar to the 27 percent average ($8,716 per capita) for the four social democratic countries in 2001.

Social spending is lower in the English-speaking democracies, and liberal welfare states make more extensive use of group-targeting and means-testing. Yet even here it is evident that benefits are considerable: in 2001, liberal democracies spent on average 17 percent of GDP, which amounted to $5,260 per capita.[2] Even in the lower-spending United States, that there is nonetheless a notably generous distribution of benefits to the aged can be seen in the $19,688 that was spent on pensions and services for each American age 65 and older.

Welfare states reduce individuals' dependence on markets as a source of well-being, and we have growing evidence attesting to the profound effects of social policy on poverty and inequality. As we noted in the introduction, welfare state spending effort is strongly connected to the subsequent level of absolute as well as relative poverty. In making a substantial dent in poverty, generous social policies mitigate the numerous and enduring effects of concentrated poverty for individuals and families. Welfare states also influence the *duration* of negative economic events for individuals (DiPrete 2002), with social policies in countries such as Sweden and Germany reducing the economic risks associated with job loss or marital dissolution.

The consequences of welfare state policies for ascriptively defined inequalities are also beginning to come into focus (Orloff 1993 a; Korpi 2000). For example, inequalities between women and men are shaped by the ways in which social policies are organized around male-breadwinner versus more egalitarian models of households. Generous welfare states also mitigate the zero-sum trade-offs women tend to otherwise face in choosing between paid employment and unpaid domestic work. The combination of these societal and individual-level impacts attests to the ways in which social policies differentiate the world's developed democracies.

The Embedded Preferences Argument

The presence of sizable levels of social provision within all developed democracies represents a remarkable historical accomplishment. It is at the very center of efforts during the past century to humanize the operation of capitalism and bring a significant measure of equality and fairness to markets and societies. In seeking to account for the origins, depth, and variability of welfare states, research to date has generated insights into the effects of demographic change, class-related factors, and political institutions and parties. But the policy preferences of citizens have received little systematic attention in welfare state scholarship. Remedying this neglect has been the purpose of this book.

The central proposition of our embedded preferences theory is that mass policy preferences are a powerful factor behind welfare state output. Mass opinion is consequential in two ways. First, the preferences of the public can exert a direct influence over governments and welfare states. This is because political incumbents and government officials seek to avoid electoral sanctions or such forms of voter disapproval as mass protests. They tend accordingly to incorporate mass opinion into social policymaking *prior* to, or independent of, a specific election.[3]

A second, *indirect* conduit of mass opinion's influence is elections. National elections provide an opportunity for the preferences of voters to shape the direction of welfare state and public policy activities through their influence on the partisan composition of national government. Social policy differences between political parties are a well-established feature in the political landscapes of developed democracies. In Sweden, for instance, conflict between the Social Democratic Party and the Moderate Party defines the terrain of postwar politics, as do significant differences between the U.S. Democrats and Republicans. The left-versus-right dimension of social policy conflict remains fundamental to OECD democracies, translating voters' alignments with political parties into the policymaking process.

The evidence we have presented in this book supports our embedded preferences argument. Starting with the challenge of accounting for cross-national variation in welfare states, we find that mass policy preferences are frequently an important factor behind wide disparities in social spending between social, Christian, and liberal democracies. By illuminating the operation of this major source of welfare state difference, these findings demonstrate how systematic attention to mass preferences can propel scholarly work in fruitful directions.

What of the recent historical dimension of overall welfare state output? Our results square well with the new wisdom concerning welfare state persistence. We find that a degree of policy stabilization and a pattern of growth within many Christian democracies were the two most common patterns of change in overall spending output of welfare states between 1980 and 2000. Retrenchment is not particularly common. During this time it has been limited to the two cases of Ireland and the Netherlands.

Our embedded preferences approach shows that policy preferences have operated as a source of persistence tendencies in overall spending effort within specific welfare states. That many national publics continue to prefer public social provision has constrained negative shifts in recent welfare state trajectories. But our analyses also establish that more extensive patterns of ideological change affecting mass policy preferences would readily have influenced the trajectory of welfare state development. The historical simulations we developed suggest that market-oriented opinion trends within Western Europe would likely have exerted retrenchment pressures on high-spending welfare states.

Looking at specific social policy domains is informative. We find specific domains such as sickness benefits and public-sector employment, compared to the overall dimension of welfare spending, to be characterized by lower policy responsiveness. Politicians tend to incorporate mass opinion into social policymaking in a global fashion, rather than adjusting each specific domain to match precisely citizen preferences. This shows why social policy restructuring and retrenchment have been more common within specific policy domains. There, the smaller degree of influence exerted by mass preferences allows interest groups to have greater influence, particularly when it comes to cash benefits entitlements.

What about mechanisms behind welfare state preferences themselves? Our results favor the *embeddedness* perspective, in which mass preferences are influenced by enduring forms of social relations as well as major institutions and the ideas around which they are organized. Our evidence suggests limits in economic explanations premised on the assumption that policy preferences are continually reevaluated at the individual level, while experiencing a pattern of extensive volatility in the aggregate. *Who* individuals are matters for their policy preferences, and institutions and social contexts confer a degree of short-term stability in aggregate opinion. But we stress again that tendencies involving inertia are far from inevitable. We present in conclusion a set of final estimates that provide further perspective on the probabilistic trajectories of both mass preferences and welfare state regimes.

Welfare State Theory

As we saw in chapter 1, previous scholarship has anticipated an impact of mass opinion. This is true for both of the leading contemporary theories of the welfare states, power resources and path dependency. But it is important to emphasize the ways in which an explicit focus on mass opinion represents a significant departure from previous theory. Our embedded preferences approach emphasizes that policy preferences are not an epiphenomenon of the attitudes of specific classes or the historical and contemporaneous influence of political parties and political institutions. They are, in their own right, an important and vital mechanism behind the operation of modern welfare states.

A key implication of our argument is that mass policy preferences may eventually transcend their historical origins. This has occurred within much of Scandinavia, where historically potent coalitions between manual workers and their allies facilitated the establishment of social democratic states in which a majority of citizens come to have a vested interest in accessing welfare benefits and services. Because this set in place a foundation for well-institutionalized preferences for public social provision, explaining the *cross*-class bases of welfare state support requires an independent focus on causal impact of mass opinion. The establishment of a broader foundation for welfare state preferences, including through collective memory processes, generates patterns of policy preferences that draw from, without reducing to, class conflicts and welfare state developments.

Our embedded preferences approach firms up a key claim of path dependency explanations concerning mechanisms behind the "locking-in" of welfare state development. Why do politicians have greater incentive to maintain (or expand) than to retrench welfare provisions? We identify mass policy attitudes as a key factor explaining the distribution of incentives among political officials, including the costs associated with the choice to pursue retrenchment. Because aggregate policy preferences are difficult to remake over short periods of time, lock-in tendencies affecting contemporary welfare states operate not only through established mechanisms such as constitutional structure, but also through the degree of aggregate support for public social provision within a country. The concept of constituencies can be usefully generalized to the public as a whole.

Contrasting with both our own approach and path dependency theorizing is scholarship arguing for convergence tendencies in social policymaking (Wilensky 2002). But we find little evidence for this bold restatement of the modernization paradigm. The average difference in the overall spending output of developed welfare states and regime types has declined only slightly, and this is entirely a product of the countries within specific types of regimes becoming more similar to one another. Furthermore, in the 1980s and 1990s, continental Christian democracies tended to adopt higher levels of spending effort. This contrasts with the European Union version of the convergence thesis.

Persistence tendencies within generous welfare states suggest serious flaws in restatements of the "end of ideology" thesis (Fukuyama 1992). Since the end of the cold war, developed democracies have not converged upon a single, market-oriented style of social policymaking. Conflicts over policy ideas and cross-national differences in mass opinion are a reality, ones that underlie the persistence of different welfare systems.

The United States in Comparative Perspective

A core expectation of democratic theory, and of much research on mass opinion, is that democratic polities *should* be characterized by responsiveness on the part of politicians to the preferences of citizens. Whether actually-existing democracies *are* characterized by policy responsiveness is the subject of recent controversies (Burstein 1998; Manza and Cook 2002).

To date, research on policy responsiveness has focused most extensively on the case of the United States. In that contentious debate (which we reviewed in chapter 1), some analysts have claimed to find a very strong relationship between opinion and policy, while others have declared the relationship to be weak or in decline. Putting the question in comparative perspective allows us to draw some fruitful new conclusions.

First, the United States is not an outlier with regard to welfare state responsiveness to mass opinion. Regarding social policy spending output as a whole, U.S. opinion/social policy linkage is in line with democratic responsiveness within other polities. By the same token, welfare state responsiveness is not by any means limited to the United States, to liberal democracies, or to countries with majoritarian political systems.

But we have unearthed evidence for some cross-national patterning in responsiveness when it comes to the specific domains of pension benefits and public health policy. In both cases, the United States and other liberal democracies are at the low end in the spectrum of responsiveness. Findings of patterning call for further scholarship, and we expect new sources of data will help to advance our understanding of variation in the autonomy of politicians and the influence of interest groups.

A further phenomenon that the U.S. case brings into focus concerns cross-national variation in the level of Americans' attitudes toward the welfare state. Even among liberal democracies, U.S. preferences for public social provision are fairly low. Our simulations have incorporated a key point about the United States in comparative perspective: low levels of public support for the welfare state are a central reason behind the market-oriented character of the American political economy. This finding will be encouraging to cross-national analysts of mass opinion, and it may constructively challenge past arguments that have asserted institutional factors to be of paramount or sole importance in accounting for American exceptionalism.

Criticisms and Counterarguments

Any novel theory of welfare states must not only generate new empirical findings, but also respond to questions or criticisms regarding underlying theoretical assumptions and causal logic. There are three lines of commentary that pose further challenges to the argument we have developed: (1) the arguments presented in "minimalist" and "critical" theories of public opinion; (2) our reliance on the aggregation of countries into welfare state regime types; and (3) claims regarding the endogenous character of mass opinion. We consider each of these in turn.

The Minimalist Portrait of Mass Opinion

Perhaps the most general potential criticism of our embedded preferences approach stems from the view that the attitudes of mass publics are simply incapable of providing an effective signal that can be processed by politicians and policymakers. Arguments to this effect have been presented in various forms within the social sciences since the early days of opinion research (e.g., Blumer 1969 [1948]; Bourdieu 1979; Ginsberg 1986; see also Herbst [1993] for a historical analysis). In the work of "critical theorists," mass opinion is highly malleable, readily subject to elite manipulation, or conditioned by the framing and contextual effects of opinion polling itself.

This line of thinking owes much of its intellectual heft to the foundational work of Converse and his colleagues' analysis and interpretation of U.S. National Election Study surveys from the 1950s and early 1960s. In *The American Voter* (1960) and also in Converse's widely cited 1964 article "The Nature of Belief Systems in Mass Publics," the Michigan scholars presented their interpretation of American public opinion as characterized by exceedingly low levels of information, political sophistication, and ideological consistency. This "minimalist view" represented an important scholarly milestone in the study of public opinion insofar as it appeared to clash decisively with both empirical democratic theory and the normative expectations of U.S. civic culture (see Sniderman et al. 1991). In calling into question the coherence of mass opinion, even the very existence of policy "attitudes" among citizens, the work of Converse and his colleagues anticipates and lends empirical justification to critical theorists' doubts regarding mass opinion.

While still the subject of important research, much of this conclusion is unwarranted. A key issue concerns limitations with the minimalist interpretation itself. A fundamental contribution of the Michigan scholars was to unearth low levels of political information among the American public, and this finding has weathered the test of time.[4] Yet high levels of information per se are neither equivalent to nor necessary for the existence of policy preferences.

Indeed, a large body of subsequent work has taken as its point of departure low information levels, demonstrating how individuals are nevertheless capable of forming and expressing politically relevant judgments, including evaluating candidates and policy options (Stoker 1992; Carmines and Huckfeldt 1996; Niemi and Weisberg 2001). Within the cognitive-psychological tradition of research that we considered in chapter 5, such common phenomena as views of group interests, patterns of affect toward political parties and institutions, and tendencies to identify with specific types of ideological labels or national slogans represent heuristics with which individuals make policy judgments (Sniderman et al. 1991). By virtue of their analytical focus on factual information and political sophistication per se, the minimalist scholars were unable to envision how habits, biases, and emotionally laden convictions provide a working foundation for policy preferences.[5]

In this context, a key innovation in contemporary work on opinion/policy linkages (e.g., Page and Shapiro 1983; Stimson et al. 1995), including our own research in this book, has been to focus on the *aggregate* level of mass opinion. For policymakers, information about the policy preferences of individuals within a population is impossible to obtain. By contrast, aggregation is readily interpretable. It is available from a wide range of polling sources and is subsequently diffused by other outlets, providing also an efficient means of filtering any non-attitudes in the public. Random guessing or nonresponses in survey research do not affect estimates of the average policy attitude. It is aggregate opinion that politicians incorporate if responsiveness indeed occurs.

Given, then, the existence of policy preferences on the part of at least some citizens, their aggregation yields an interpretable signal for policymakers. This is most likely on issues in which there are already well-defined differences between parties and other organizations, so that political leadership may provide a subsequent means of translating mass attitudes into policy (Shapiro 1998). The ideological content of aggregate opinion, as well as its degree of influence over policy output, may vary over time and across national context. But questions about the magnitude of this variation can be answered only through empirical research. The minimalist portrait of mass opinion, as well as less formal statements to this effect, provides no valid basis for ruling out the existence of policy preferences or a significant pattern of influence over policymaking.

The Classification of Welfare States and Regime Types

A second point of potential controversy stems from our use of aggregated *types* of welfare states (see also Arts and Gelissen 2002). Our classification of welfare states raises two relevant questions: First, is the threefold liberal/Christian democratic/social democratic scheme inferior to alternatives? Second, are all attempts at regime classifications ultimately misleading, given the existence of cross-national differences between welfare states classified *within* a single regime type?

Starting with the first issue, the threefold typology first introduced by Esping-Andersen (1990) continues to be the most influential way of identifying the main features distinguishing welfare states across different world regions. This typology provides a point of departure and comparison with earlier work. But, remarkably after all the scrutiny it has received, the Esping-Andersen scheme and its variants continue to yield fruitful summaries of social policy differences.[6] For example, *between-regime* differences in welfare state effort continue to be notably larger than *within-regime* differences involving individual countries. Using the most recent year of full OECD data (2001), the standard deviation of welfare spending effort for the three regime types is 4.1 percage pointst, in comparison to *within-regime* differences for social, Christian, and liberal democracies of 2.8, 3.1 percent, and 2.6 percentage points, respectively. Within-regime differences are thus smaller than between-regime differences.

This does not, however, rule out the possibility that alternative schemes may prove useful in formulating and answering other questions (see, e.g., Korpi and Palme 1998). For example, a number of analysts have proposed that the heterogeneity of liberal democracies creates a rationale for separately classifying Australia and New Zealand as members of an additional regime type (Castles and Mitchell 1993). Clearly this classification may be useful in its own right, though its relevance in our application appears low. For instance, the 2001 OECD data show that deletion of Australia and New Zealand actually *increases* within-liberal-democracy heterogeneity, because these two countries have spending values close to the within-regime average.

Perhaps a more fundamental objection is whether *any* classification of welfare states is valid or analytically desirable, given the existence of cross-national differences within regime types. This objection appears to be particularly common among scholars outside the comparative welfare state tradition, yet it risks abandoning the criterion of parsimony. Indeed, absent some conceptual scheme for classification, scholars would be left with no grounds for identifying or otherwise appreciating any ideal-typical clustering of welfare states.

Cross-national comparisons between specific countries are, of course, important and informative.[7] The analyses we have presented in this book have sought accordingly to strike a balance with respect to between-regime and between-country comparisons. Yet the utility of balancing between fine-grained analyses and ideal-type comparisons again underscores the analytical value of the regime concept. The possibility of more useful classification or measurement schemes emerging in the future should not be ruled out. But the main challenge for welfare state research is not to reflexively banish all simplifying devices.

Mass Policy Preferences, Endogeneity, and Causal Inference

The third line of objection we consider is the thesis that because mass policy preferences are ultimately endogenous, they cannot be considered a fundamental ingredient in explanations of welfare state activity. In its most specific and technical meaning, *endogeneity* refers to an association between a right-hand-side variable and an unobserved error term (Wooldridge 2002: chap. 4). This most commonly results from simultaneity bias or reverse causation, in which the explanatory variable is affected by the dependent variable. Contemporaneous policy "feedback" is one example of this scenario (Weir et al. 1988a; Thelen 1999), and this idea has been used at times to argue sweepingly against the preferences of the public as a factor behind government activity. Yet, as we discussed in chapter 1, other strains of scholarship have instead anticipated the policy influence of mass opinion, defining a key point of scholarly disagreement.

Is the interrelationship of mass policy preferences and welfare state policies characterized by endogeneity? Although critics have sometimes framed the issue as reflecting a settled consensus, it represents an empirical question, one marked by the absence of relevant evidence. Claims regarding endogeneity should thus be seen as hypotheses in need of suitable evaluation.

Our applications of Hausman's (1978) test provide a means of empirically addressing the issue. The results we presented in chapter 2 deliver evidence *against* endogeneity bias and the operation of short-term policy feedback. While mass policy preferences clearly influence welfare states, spending output does not simultaneously shape policy preferences. This means that welfare states' influence on mass opinion operates with long lags, a point we have incorporated into our approach through the collective-memory thesis.

In the face of these results, a second and quite different thesis is that *other* theoretically relevant factors behind welfare states influence mass policy preferences (e.g., Immergut 1998). Of course, most welfare state factors have some degree of interrelationship, and a central virtue of multivariate analyses is to parcel out their respective degree of influence over welfare state output. In seeking to establish mass policy preferences as a causal factor behind welfare states, we have followed standard practice by taking into account other potentially confounding sources of welfare state output.

We treated policy preferences as themselves subject to explanation in chapter 5, in our investigation of sources of welfare state attitudes. But looking at preferences as an outcome to be explained is distinct from the endogeneity scenario. Our embedded preferences approach argues for social structure, major institutions, and collective memory as factors behind comparative-historical variation in preferences. Again, this should not be taken as implying that mass policy preferences cannot be a causal factor with respect to welfare state policies at one point in time. Rather, it means that mass policy preferences, like any causal factor, possess their own prior foundations.[8]

Welfare State Trajectories

Finally, we turn to the implications of our analysis for the future of the welfare state. Public support for maintaining welfare states provides a key source of resistance to retrenchment pressures within many countries. Stabilization trends within Scandinavia and growing levels of welfare spending effort within many Christian democracies during the 1990s are especially notable. That citizens within these high-spending polities tend to endorse their continuation, in spite of recurring declarations of "crisis," helps us to understand the contemporary foundations of welfare states.

But persistence tendencies within many welfare states do not make for an inevitable future. Welfare policies are shaped by multiple sources of pressure. The cases of Ireland and the Netherlands show that factors other than mass policy preferences can, at times, be enough to facilitate retrenchment, even in the face of persisting public support. Regarding policy preferences, we have argued that tendencies involving inertia are probabilistic in nature, and therein subject to further pressures toward change. The exercise of statistical modeling reminds us that there is an intrinsically random component in public policymaking. Wars, economic crises, social movement conflicts, and new policy visions are certain to appear in the future and disrupt the status quo in ways that cannot be anticipated.

Given the probabilistic and multicausal nature of social policymaking, what implications do our findings have for future trajectories of welfare state development? Using our statistical model of welfare effort, we consider four distinct scenarios. Each of these scenarios represents an extension of current trends or, alternatively, a historical event that comes to influence an established factor behind social policymaking:

(1) Demographic convergence in which developed democracies come to resemble the country (Norway) that we forecast as having the largest proportion of working women (among countries for which we have sufficient data to make out-of-sample predictions).

(2) A pattern of economic growth in which all developed democracies become similarly more affluent. We simulate this scenario by assuming that developed democracies come to attain the U.S. level of per capita GDP.

(3) Ideological trends in which mass opinion within countries converges on the Norwegian level of policy preferences, due to a new pattern of transnational influence, or to a similar response by institutional leaders that diffuses cross-nationally.

(4) Ideological trends in which mass opinion within countries converges on the U.S. level of policy preferences, due to a new pattern of transnational influence, or to a similar response by institutional leaders that diffuses cross-nationally.

We examine these scenarios through simulations in which we alter, in turn, the level of a relevant independent variable in accordance with each scenario. We compare forecasts for each scenario against an initial baseline prediction. This baseline prediction is the predicted level of welfare spending effort for each country in 2015 according to our statistical model of the ISSP/OECD data. Baseline estimates are derived by first estimating the linear rate of over-time change in all covariates, repeating these calculations for each country. This enables us to estimate country-specific covariate levels for the time period (2015) with respect to which we wish to forecast welfare state spending effort. Using the latter values and the co-efficient estimates from our statistical model, we then derive the predicted level of welfare state effort for specific countries.[9]

Estimates for Norway are presented in figure 7.1. The baseline estimate is in the left panel. Here, the initial forecast is for Norwegian welfare spending to grow from 25 percent of GDP in 1997 to 30 percent by 2015.

How might this baseline be altered if Norway experiences the four scenarios we have outlined? The first scenario of demographic change (estimate 1) uses Norwegian index values, so it is identical to the baseline forecast. But the second scenario (estimate 2), where Norway experiences the U.S. level of economic development, shows a divergent trend. This trend enhances the Norwegian welfare state's predicted growth, because by 2015, economic development level in Norway is forecast as two percentage points *higher* than in the United States.

Scenarios 3 and 4 consider the influence of trends involving the level of mass policy preferences. Scenario 3 uses the predicted Norwegian level of policy preferences, and thus yields identical estimates to the baseline prediction. But in scenario 4, a trend toward the U.S. level of policy preferences reduces Norwegian welfare state output to 23 percent in 2015. This

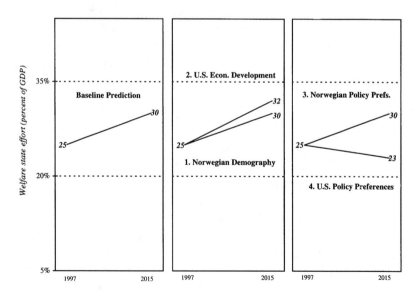

FIGURE 7.1. Forecasting welfare state effort, Norway.

represents a massive impact, one in which aggregate opinion change transforms welfare state growth into a pattern of retrenchment.

Turning to the case of Germany in figure 7.2, the baseline forecast is for relatively stable welfare spending through 2015. A trend toward Norwegian demography (scenario 1) adds four percentage points to the baseline, whereas a trend toward the U.S. level of economic development (scenario 2) reduces German welfare state growth by four percentage points. The next pair of scenarios have similarly dramatic effects. The scenario 3 trend toward higher levels of policy preferences adds three percentage points to German welfare state growth. The trend in scenario 4 toward the U.S. level of preferences transforms the baseline prediction into a four-percentage point-decline in welfare output.

In figure 7.3, the U.S. welfare state is forecast as growing by three percentage points by 2015. Using scenario 1, a trend toward Norwegian demographic composition adds two percentage points to the baseline, and scenario 2 leaves the baseline intact. The trend in scenario 3 toward the Norwegian level of policy preferences is forecast as having a large effect, adding an additional seven percentage points to the baseline trend. Like scenario 2, the fourth scenario uses U.S. predicted values and is thus identical to the baseline estimate.

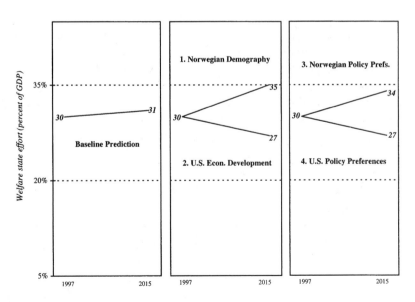

FIGURE 7.2. Forecasting welfare state effort, Germany.

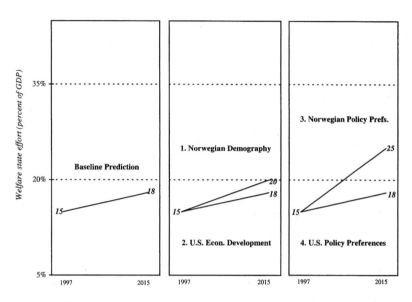

FIGURE 7.3. Forecasting welfare state effort, United States.

Final Implications

Scenarios involving this magnitude of change have not, of course, occurred. But they represent trends that can readily be envisioned. For instance, the possibility of a broad movement by citizens within capitalist democracies toward a greater preference for private social provision is not inconceivable. Economic affluence, as exemplified in popular portrayals of the contemporary United States, is a powerful stimulus for emulation among both policymakers and ordinary citizens. Individualistic visions of markets and societies are clearly present to some degree within all democracies. Further, the expansion of anti-immigrant or racist views, especially when connected more closely to individualistic policy attitudes, might enhance receptivity to nativist social movements or calls for welfare reform.

By the same token, however, many of these historical processes may conceivably exert a different influence. Rather than enhancing the attractiveness of neoliberalism, cautionary tales regarding the downside of unregulated markets potentially fuel risk aversion and skepticism. The growing presence of immigrant groups within most democracies could expand constituencies for social benefits and services, particularly if the group members are not deprived of political rights or excluded by left and religious parties. Growing understanding of the trade-off between solidaristic social democracies and individualistic liberal democracies may remind citizens within high-spending polities of their vested interests in maintaining access to cradle-to-grave entitlements. Lower levels of public provisions in liberal democracies may serve as an indicator of the unwelcome presence of poverty and inequality that tend to follow in the wake of retrenchment and privatization.

In this context, persistence tendencies within social-democratic welfare states are again of programmatic importance. So too are trends involving rising spending effort among many Christian democracies during the 1990s. The emergence of a recognizable European style of public provision may serve as an ideological resource for welfare state supporters. When combined with strategic efforts by sympathetic politicians and activists on behalf of welfare states, a more distinctly European model of welfare could eventually give rise to new linkages between national or regional identity and public policy preferences, buttressing existing social policy arrangements (see also Kautto et al. 2001b; Rifkin 2004).

In coming years, these considerations may complement the social and institutional factors behind contemporary pressures toward inertia in aggregate policy preferences, making contraction in cross-national differences between welfare states unlikely. Rather than a world of homogeneous policy regimes, the contemporary historical era is one of markedly different welfare states and types of societies. National configurations of mass policy preferences have been critical to the robustness of many West European welfare states during this time. They will likely be implicated in any future transformations.

Notes

Introduction

1. On reducing income inequality, see Ringen and Uusitalo 1992; Korpi and Palme 1998; Page and Simmons 2000; and Bradley et al. 2003. On poverty, see Kenworthy 1999; Huber and Stephens 2001, chap. 4; and Brady 2003a, b.

2. Within the welfare state literatures, spending "effort" measures of this type have been the most common measure of overall social welfare output. There are alternative measures of welfare state provision, and we consider these in greater detail in subsequent chapters. But welfare effort measures are important, because they have been used in most of the recent and pathbreaking research on welfare state effects on stratification.

3. Examples abound. See, for example, Monroe 1998; Page and Shapiro 1983; Erikson, MacKuen, and Stimson. 2002a, b; see also Hill, Leighley, and Hinton-Andersson 1995 and Berry, Ringquist, Fording, and Hanson 1998 for studies of subnational policy responsiveness.

4. To date, a small number of studies of opinion/policy linkages have been conducted for countries other than the United States (see Brooks 1987, 1990; Petry 1999; Soroka and Wlezien 2004, 2005). These innovative studies have broached comparative questions about opinion/policy linkages in democracies, yet their use of measures that vary across country context raises new questions about the impact of the country-specific measures themselves. Two studies have sought to use cross-nationally comparable measures (see Alesina and Glaesar 2004, chap. 7; Mehrtens 2004), and they have reached different conclusions regarding the policy influence of mass opinion. We discuss in chapter 2 the methodological promise as well as limitations of past studies.

5. On the origins of this concept and its application to understanding social network and contextual factors behind economic outcomes, see, for example, Granovetter 1985, 1995, 2005; Uzzi 1997; and Guillen et al. 2002.

Chapter One

1. The Christian-democratic welfare state has at times been characterized as "conservative" (Esping-Andersen 1990) as a means of capturing its institutional reliance on traditional ideas about gender, including the historical use of family support to buttress a male-breadwinner model of the labor force.

2. See Herbst (1998) for an analysis of how politicians access and interpret public opinion.

3. It is notable that in spite of their criticisms of polls and surveys as measures of public opinion, some critical theorists have nonetheless acknowledged that poll-based influences on policymaking are more democratic than some other representations of public views (see, e.g., Lewis 2001: 28–29). The most prominent of these alternatives are the mass media, which are usually far less representative and closed to the public than opinion polls, as critical theorists acknowledge (e.g., Bennett and Entman 2001).

4. Research on voting behavior provides evidence that ordinary voters are capable of ideological or policy-oriented evaluations of candidates and incumbents. Whereas early research suggested that low levels of factual information among voters made such behavior unlikely (Campbell, Converse, Miller, and Stokes 1960; Converse 1964), the thrust of recent work is that voters do not necessarily need extensive information (Carmines and Huckfeldt 1996; Lupia, McCubbins, and Popkin 2000; Brooks, Manza, and Bolzendahl 2003). Instead, voters routinely combine their preferences with attributions about the past or future positions and activities of incumbents, candidates, or parties to form subsequent judgments (Kiewiet 1983; Alvarez and Nagler 1998). This exemplifies the use by citizens of habits, biases, and emotionally laden convictions in political reasoning and decision-making (Sniderman, Brody, and Tetlock 1991).

5. We emphasize that the existence of cross-national differences in mass policy preferences is by itself insufficient to provide direct evidence of a relationship. One reason individual-level opinion surveys are intrinsically limited is that they do not directly measure welfare state outcomes (or other country-level processes). A second reason is that analysis of opinion and other individual-level data cannot incorporate controls for confounding, country-level processes such as economic development level or constitutional structures. But see Mehrtens (2004) for one study that provides evidence for a link between measures of mass opinion and the level of welfare state decommodification.

Chapter Two

1. Within the comparative welfare state literature, Australia and New Zealand have sometimes been conceptualized as members of a "radical" regime type separa-

ble from the liberal regime (Castles and Mitchell 1993), though these two countries share with other English-speaking democracies a greater use of means-testing, and also considerable similarity with respect to welfare state institutions. This is not, of course, to say that a separate classification of the Antipodes would not be useful in other research applications.

2. Effort-related measures can be subject to denominator effects, as when inflation-adjusted spending levels are constant but a growing economy means that effort-based measures show a declining trend. Scenarios of this sort are, however, best construed as indicative of real decline, insofar as it is *relative* spending that ultimately matters for understanding inequality. Further, we would expect social spending to keep pace with changes in a society's level of productivity if aggregate welfare output is indeed stable over time (see also Swank 2002).

3. Surveys of specific countries for a given ISSP module were not always fielded in the same calendar year, so the coding of country-years in the analysis reflects the actual year of the survey.

4. See Mehrtens (2004) for an important exception to the tendency for opinion analysts to ignore measures of welfare output. In particular, Mehrtens's study provides evidence linking mass policy preferences to Esping-Andersen's measure of welfare decommodification.

5. A second possibility raised by Alesina and Glaesar's (2004) work is that the relationship between mass opinion and social policymaking might be subject to endogeneity bias. This issue and the results of our specification testing are discussed at greater length below and in the chapter's appendix.

6. The frequency of referenda is sometimes used in constructing measures of veto points, but in our ISSP/OECD dataset all but one country-year scores "0," rendering this variable uninformative.

7. As summarized in table 2.2, the *Comparative Welfare States Dataset* (Huber et al. 2004) provides measures of partisan control over government. Our final analyses drop the variable measuring right party control, and this exclusion has no impact on results.

8. We do not include a measure of union density in the analysis. Recent data on comparative unionization rates are sparse, particularly for liberal democracies in the period since the mid-1990s (see Visser 1996; Ebbinghaus and Visser 2000), and any attempt to include unionization data would require us to drop nearly half the current observations from our primary dataset. But in keeping with earlier scholarship, because there is a strong association between left party strength and union density (Huber and Stephens 2001), our inability to include a covariate for union density is of limited consequence.

9. A further version of the Huber-White approach is the HC3 estimator. A Monte Carlo analysis by Long and Ervin (2000) finds this approach to perform well in small samples characterized by heteroskedasticity. In the current application, the HC3 estimator deliverers comparable results to the robust-cluster approach,

though in several cases standard errors are slightly smaller using HC3. The latter discrepancy may be a product of the HC3 estimator not taking into account correlated errors within clusters, a point noted by Moller et al. (2003).

10. With reference to country-level data, the fixed-effects approach has a further unfortunate consequence discussed by Beck and Katz (2001). In essence, by including dummy variables for countries to condition on unit-specific "fixed effects," this approach yields explanations that "control," for instance, for "Sweden being Sweden" and "the United Kingdom being the United Kingdom." This again contrasts with the setup for longitudinal individual-level data, where the ith survey respondent is generally not of theoretical interest, and might be more readily regarded as a nuisance parameter to be controlled in multivariate analysis.

11. That mass policy preferences are simultaneously influenced by other (measured) independent variables is to be expected, yet this is not an instance of endogeneity bias. It is taken into account by inclusion of controls in a multivariate model.

12. A similar consideration applies to analysis of the potential interrelationship between mass policy preferences and cumulative years of Christian-democratic party governance. This yields an estimate of 3.33 (s.e. = .49) for the main effects of mass policy preferences on overall welfare output, a larger estimate than in model 2.

13. Decomposition methods extend regression analysis, using coefficient estimates and time- or group-specific levels of independent variables, to calculate the relative or absolute contribution of covariates to explaining differences in the dependent variable. Decomposition analysis has often been applied to between-group comparisons in expected earnings, labor-force participation, and aggregate change in mass opinion. See Firebaugh (1997) for further discussion using a variety of datasets to illustrate techniques.

14. Note that *observed* differences in table 2.4 for welfare state effort in social versus liberal democracies (*+11 percent*) are presented in italics to differentiate these quantities from the decomposition estimates.

Chapter Three

1. Further turning the "pessimistic" view of economic globalization on its head, such long-term economic transformations as the declining share of manufacturing employment may actually exert pressures for greater welfare state provisions within many developed democracies (Iversen 2001).

2. These would include studies of France (Palier 2001), Italy (Ferrera 1997), Germany (Bonker and Wollmann 2001), Japan (Estevez-Abe 2002), New Zealand and Australia (Castles 1996), Sweden (Anderson 2001; Timonen 2001), Switzerland (Bonoli 2001),the United Kingdom (Ginsburg 2001; Taylor-Gooby 2001), and the United States (Bashevkin 2000; Weaver 2000).

3. See also Korpi (2003, 2004) and Korpi and Palme (2003) for parallel work on welfare entitlements, but using indices of replacement income not yet released in the public domain.

4. Formally, these analyses involve counterfactual inference, an analytic strategy that is gaining in application within the social sciences (e.g., Kiser and Levi 1996; Dinardo and Lemieux 1997; Alderson 1999), particularly among quantitative analysts. In the current study, we seek to incorporate methodological criteria identified by scholars as central to valid applications of counterfactual analysis (Tetlock and Belkin 1996; cf. Hawthorne 1991). Most important of these are *clarity* (specifying the variables under consideration); *historical consistency* (maximizing plausibility by minimizing the number of counterfactuals simultaneously considered); and *statistical consistency* (developing inferences based on analysis of real data).

5. In this context, we emphasize that our statistical model takes into account potentially confounding factors influencing the historical trajectory of welfare states, including such retrenchment-constraining forces as women's labor force participation.

6. As discussed in note 4, this approach maximizes the plausibility of the simulations by developing inferences that are based on real data, rather than the use of country/time-specific covariate levels that are speculative. The simulation analysis involves, then, substitution of one country's covariate level for another's. In contrast, a more ambitious but less plausible simulation would be one in which the manipulation involves covariate levels that are not observed for any country-year.

7. For these analyses, we use Norway as an exemplar of the social democratic regime type, since the ISSP/OECD dataset contains data on Sweden only for 1997 (see table 3.1).

Chapter Four

1. To be sure, the fact that few charter members were able to fully meet this fiscal requirement during the 1990s underscores the potential complexity (and possibly limited influence) of this aspect of EU influence on European welfare states.

2. Consider, for instance, a comparison between two hypothetical regime types, each composed of a pair of countries, where the initial welfare state values for the two countries composing the first type are, respectively, 15 percent and 25 percent, and the initial welfare state values for the second pair of countries are, respectively, 20 percent and 30 percent. The average *between-country* difference is, then, 5.6 percentage points, and the average *between-regime* difference is 2.5. The *within-regime* difference for both regime types is 5 percentage points.

Consider now the further possibility that at a subsequent point in time, values for the pair of countries within the first regime type are stable at 15 percent and 25 percent, whereas values for the pair of countries composing the second regime type are 23 percent and 27 percent. The average *between-country* difference is now 4.6

percentage points, revealing a substantial decline from the initial value of 5.6 percent. But regarding *between-regime* differences, these show no change over time, remaining steady at 2.5 percent. Rounding out this picture, *within-regime* differences for the first type are unchanged, but within-regime differences for the second are now 2 percentage points, establishing a growing similarity over time among the countries composing the second regime. Calculations of this sort reveal the potential complexity of over-time patterns of change in welfare state differences, and thus the importance of systematically measuring these distinct dimensions of cross-national variation.

Chapter Five

1. It should be emphasized that when Downs (1957) presented his manifesto for an economic model of political behavior, he did so during an era in which the mass society portrait of individuals as seemingly helpless in the face of elite influence was dominant (cf. Kornhauser 1959). Consistent with the mass society perspective, assumptions regarding low levels of ideological constraint or sophistication among the public led to predictions of randomness in individual and aggregate opinion (e.g., Campbell, Converse, Miller, and Stokes 1960; Converse 1964). Economic approaches constituted a distinct alternative to such models, at both the individual and aggregate levels.

2. This further assumption is central to the economic approach. As will become clearer in the course of our discussion, self-interest without maximizing/updating of preferences leads to a portrait of voters as indifferent to economic change once their preferences are initially established, a view potentially consistent with non-economic approaches.

3. See, e.g., Alt and Chrystal (1983); Popkin (1991); Sniderman, Brody, and Tetlock (1991); see also Kahneman, Slovic, and Tversky (1982).

4. Whereas the effects of mass opinion on policy output are estimated by measuring mass opinion using a one-year lag, Erikson et al. (2002a: chap. 9) estimate the effects of public policy on mass opinion with no lag in the public policy covariate.

5. Lipset's account of social cleavages is compatible with two quite different accounts of over-time patterns of political and ideological change. In one early characterization, Lipset and Rokkan (1967) offered their well-known prediction that institutionalized patterns of partisan political conflict were essentially "frozen" in the historical era of the 1950s. In subsequent work, Lipset (1983: chap. 14) offered the modified argument that changes in social cleavages affecting key segments of national populations were steadily transforming electoral politics within capitalist democracies. Despite some obvious differences, an important point of similarity is that both interpretations rely upon underlying assumptions about social structure as a key source of citizens' preferences.

6. As a causal factor behind aggregate opinion, social cleavages can operate at multiple levels in ways that may (or may not) complement one another. Taking recent work on the economic asset-bases of attitudes as an example, Iversen and Soskice (2001) argue that the degree to which individuals possess skills requiring extensive training shapes their level of preference for social insurance protections. Skilled manual workers or credentialed professionals, then, will often be an important source of aggregate welfare state support, and cross-national variation in the distribution of a skill-intensive workforce can contribute to between-country differences in welfare state attitudes.

7. For further analyses, see Nunn, Crockett, and Williams (1978); Sullivan, Pierson and Marcus (1982); and Smith (1990a).

8. This sociological portrait of policy attitudes was further refined by McClosky and his colleagues (McClosky and Brill 1983; McClosky and Zaller 1984). Focusing on questions about public support for an array of democratic principles and policies, these scholars argued that American policy attitudes were also linked to various occupational and organizational groups, each of which tend to emphasize distinct ideological positions or norms. For instance, whereas the teaching and legal professions were assumed to be organized around civil libertarian goals, law enforcement and business occupations were seen as considerably more willing to restrict liberties for the sake of maintaining order. Like cohort replacement processes or change in the educational level of the American public, the relative size of occupations and voluntary associations tends to change slowly over time, operating as a stabilizing force on aggregate opinion.

9. A large literature on collective memory has sprouted up in recent years. For some important contributions, see, e.g., Schwartz (2000), Fine (2001), Olick (2003), and Zerubavel (2003).

10. It is worth noting that early formulations of the economic approach (see Kramer 1983) explicitly rejected the concept of sociotropic evaluations, arguing also against the validity of individual-level measures of voters' policy preferences as a means of understanding economically motivated political behavior. Contemporary reformulations of the economic approach, including Erickson et al.'s (2002a) important work, explicitly embrace the concept of sociotropic evaluations, arguing for the subjectivity of economically motivated behavior (i.e., where economic change is mediated by voters' evaluations).

11. Duch, Palmer, and Anderson (2000) present evidence concerning the magnitude of ecological inference bias under these conditions, illustrating the significant risks of relying on purely aggregate-level measures of economic factors when analyzing individual-level outcomes.

12. To facilitate comparisons in this figure as well as in subsequent analyses, we have rescaled all items to a range of 0–1, with higher scores indicating greater support for welfare state programs and policies.

13. Regarding coefficient estimates for the effects of economic evaluations, six

out of a total of eight coefficients are significant. These six are for sociotropic and egocentric evaluations in the United States (β = .02, s.e. < .01; β = .02, s.e. < .01), sociotropic evaluations in Sweden (β= –.04, s.e. = .01), sociotropic evaluations in Norway (β= –.01, s.e. < .01), and sociotropic and egocentric evaluations in the Netherlands (β= .04, s.e. = .01; β = .02, s.e. = .01). While most coefficients for the parallel effects of social cleavage and institutional factors are also significant, we postpone a more detailed discussion of the relative magnitude of economic versus sociological factors to the next subsection.

14. This is achieved by holding constant the two economic evaluation variables at their respective means for 1976, the first year in the analysis of the welfare state benefits item.

15. These comparisons involve both continuous and categorical covariates. For continuous covariates, we calculate predicted values across the full range of a variable; for categorical covariates, we calculate predicted values using the dummy variables for smallest versus largest effects.

16. Education has a strong and negative effect on policy preferences, with higher levels of education disposing individuals to oppose welfare state benefits. To facilitate visual comparison between this effect and the others summarized in Figure 5.9, we present predicted scores by taking the absolute value of the (negatively signed) coefficient for education.

17. Given the negative sign of the coefficient for sociotropic evaluations, we again facilitate comparisons between independent variables by taking the absolute value of this coefficient (and also for the coefficient for education).

18. We stress that the key difference between economic versus embedded preferences models is not that one emphasizes "self-interest" over "symbolic" motivations. This distinction need not be explicitly carved with respect to either approach; indeed, it is one we have deliberately sought to avoid in our characterization of the embedded preferences approach. Instead, the central point of divergence concerns whether macroeconomic factors, in the form of economic evaluations, are the central source of the policy preferences, or instead one among many such sources.

Chapter Six

1. We emphasize that our coefficient estimates are based on a measure of mass policy preferences that does *not* vary across separate policy domains. As discussed earlier, this represents one of the two distinct ways in which domain-specific patterns of responsiveness can occur, where the other involves politicians responding to voter preferences that are themselves specific to domains (e.g., Soroka and Wlezian 2005). Limitations as well as benefits of this nonvarying measure of policy preferences are discussed below.

2. The full standardization of the coefficients means that a more exact summary

of predicted effects is that a single deviation increase in policy preferences raises by .50 standard deviations the level of welfare state effort. To avoid cumbersome language, our discussion of the magnitude of these and other standardized coefficients in this chapter leaves this implicit.

Chapter Seven

1. Per capita estimates of overall welfare state and domain-specific spending use purchasing power parity-adjusted calculations (PPP) to enhance cross-national comparability. All comparisons are derived from the OECD's *Social Expenditures Database.*

2. This amount does not include publicly subsidized *private* benefits that are restricted to specific categories of employees, and which are highly developed within countries such as the United States (see also Hacker 2002).

3. While arguably less common, it is also possible that political officials simply acknowledge the signals conveyed by public preferences as *legitimate,* incorporating them into social policymaking not simply to avoid voter sanctions (see also Meyer et al. 1997; Campbell 2002). The state of empirical democratic theory scholarship is such that investigating these scenarios in greater detail is in order.

4. In the most comprehensive study to date, Delli Carpini and Keeter (1996) find *no* evidence of change in the average level of Americans' political information from the 1950s to the 1990s. Likewise, there is little doubt that information level itself influences preferences and behavior (Althaus 1998). For instance, Bartels's (1996) analyses provide evidence that higher levels of information would likely benefit challengers as well as Republican candidates in U.S. presidential elections.

5. Campbell et al. (1960) explicitly discounted survey respondents' frequent reference to group interests, including reports that specific policies reflected the interests of ordinary Americans or members of their segment of society. In assuming that such judgments were free of ideological content or political relevance, the Michigan scholars missed a critical opportunity to observe the theoretically important influence of social groups on mass policy preferences (see also Lane 1962).

6. There is little reason to expect that the regime concept must always be useful in capturing cross-national differences. See, e.g., Lapinski, Riemann, Shapiro, Stevens, and Jacobs (1998) for evidence that assessments of subjective well-being vary little across regimes.

7. See, for example, the early work of Esping-Andersen (1978, 1985) on the social democratic countries, or the more recent work of O'Connor et al. (1999) on liberal democratic welfare states. See DiPrete and McManus (2000), McManus and DiPrete (2001), and Gangl (2004) for comparisons between the cases of Germany and the United States.

8. The plural foundations of mass policy preferences are worth emphasizing with

respect to recent work by Alesina and Glaesar (2004, chap. 7). Recall that chapter 2 showed no evidence that opinion/social policy linkages should vanish when the policy influence of political parties and institutions are taken into account. A *longer-term* pattern of influence by political factors on mass preferences is, of course, entirely consistent with the argument we have presented. Our embedded preferences approach potentially diverges from Alesina and Glaesar's in emphasizing that the political environment is but one of numerous social institutions that influence the formation and trajectory of policy preferences concerning the welfare state.

9. We focus on three countries for which we have complete ISSP/OECD data in 1991 and 1997 with which to predict 2015 levels of welfare effort: Germany, Norway, and the United States.

References

Aarts, Kees, Henk van der Kolk, and Marlies Kamp. 1999. *Dutch Parliamentary Election Study, 1998*. Machine-readable datafiles and codebook. Amsterdam: NIWI-Steinmetz Archive/Ann Arbor, MI: Inter-university Consortium for Political and Social Research.

Alderson, Arthur. 1999. "Explaining Deindustrialization: Globalization, Failure, or Success?" *American Sociological Review* 64:701–21.

Alesina, Alberto, and Edward Glaesar. 2004. *Fighting Poverty in the U.S. and Europe: A World of Difference*. New York: Oxford University Press.

Allan, James, and Lyle Scruggs. 2004. "Political Partisanship and Welfare State Reform in Advanced Industrial Societies." *American Journal of Political Science* 48:496–512.

Alt, James, and K. Alec Chrystal. 1983. *Political Economics*. Brighton, UK: Wheatsheaf.

Alvarez, Michael, and Jonathan Nagler. 1998. "Economics, Entitlements, and Social Issues: Voter Choice in the 1996 Presidential Election." *American Journal of Political Science* 42:1349–63.

Althaus, Scott. 1998. "Information Effects in Collective Preferences." *American Political Science Review* 92:545–58.

Amenta, Edwin, Chris Bonastia, and Neal Caren. 2001. "US Social Policy in Comparative and Historical Perspective: Concepts, Images, Arguments, and Research Strategies." *Annual Review of Sociology* 27:213–34.

Andersen, Jorgen Goul, Per Arnt Pettersen, Stefan Svallfors, and Hannu Uusitalo. 1999. "The Legitimacy of the Nordic Welfare States: Trends, Variations and Cleavages." In *Nordic Social Policy: Changing Welfare States*. Edited by Mikko Kautto, Matti Heikkilä, Bjørn Hvinden, Staffan Marklund and Niels Ploug, 235–61. New York: Routledge.

Anderson, Karen. 2001. "The Politics of Retrenchment in a Social Democratic Welfare State: Reform of Swedish Pension and Unemployment Insurance." *Comparative Political Studies* 34:1063–91.

Anker, Hans, and E. V. Oppenhuis. 1994. *Dutch Parliamentary Election Study, 1989.* Machine-readable datafiles and codebook. Amsterdam: Steinmetz Archive/ Ann Arbor, MI: Inter-university Consortium for Political and Social Research.

———. 1997. *Dutch Parliamentary Election Study, 1994.* Machine-readable datafiles and codebook). Amsterdam: Steinmetz Archive/Ann Arbor, MI: Inter-university Consortium for Political and Social Research.

Arter, David. 1999. *Scandinavian Politics Today.* New York: Manchester University Press.

Arts, Wil, and John Gelissen. 2001. "Welfare States, Solidarity and Justice Principles: Does the Type Really Matter?" *Acta Sociologica* 44:283–99.

———. 2002. "Three Worlds of Welfare Capitalism or More? A State-of-the-Art Report." *Journal of European Social Policy* 12:137–58.

Barnes, Samuel, and Max Kaase. 1983. *Political Action: An Eight Nation Study, 1973–1976.* Machine-readable data file and codebook. Ann Arbor, MI: Inter-university Consortium for Political and Social Research.

Bartels, Larry M. 1996. "Uninformed Votes: Information Effects in Presidential Elections." *American Journal of Political Science* 40:194–230.

Bartolini, Stefano, and Peter Mair. 1990. *Identity, Competition, and Electoral Availability.* New York: Cambridge University Press.

Bashevkin, Sylvia. 2000. "Rethinking Retrenchment: North American Social Policy during the Early Clinton and Chretien Years." *Canadian Journal of Political Science* 33:7–36.

Beck, Nathaniel, and Jonathan Katz. 1995. "What to Do (and Not to Do) with Time-Series Cross-Section Data." *American Political Science Review* 89:634–47.

———. 2001. "Throwing Out the Baby with the Bathwater: A Comment on Green, Kim, and Yoon." *International Organization* 55:487–95.

Bell, Daniel. 1973. *The Coming of Post-Industrial Society.* New York: Basic Books.

Bennett, W. Lance, and Robert Entman, eds. 2001. *Mediated Politics.* New York: Cambridge University Press.

Berger, Suzanne. 2000. "Globalization and Politics." *Annual Review of Political Science* 3:43–62.

Berry, William, Evan Ringquist, Richard Fording, and Russell Hanson. 1998. "Measuring Citizen and Government Ideology in the American States, 1960–1993." *American Journal of Political Science* 42:327–48.

Beveridge, William Henry. 1960[1944]. *Full Employment in a Free Society: A Report.* 2nd ed. London: Allen and Unwin.

Blau, Peter M., and Otis Dudley Duncan. 1967. *The American Occupational Structure.* New York: Wiley.

Blekesaune, Martin, and Jill Quadagno. 2003. "Public Attitudes toward Welfare State Policies: A Comparative Analysis of 24 Nations." *European Sociological Review* 19:415–27.

Block, Fred. 1977. "The Ruling Class Does Not Rule." *Socialist Review* 33:6–28.

Blumer, Herbert. 1948. "Public Opinion and Public Opinion Polling." *American Sociological Review* 13:542–54.

———. 1969. *Symbolic Interactionism: Perspective and Method.* Englewood Cliffs, NJ: Prentice-Hall.

Bonker, Frank, and Hellmut Wollmann. 2001. "Stumbling towards Reform: The German Welfare State in the 1990s." In *Welfare States under Pressure.* Edited by Peter Taylor-Gooby, 75–99. Thousand Oaks, CA: Sage.

Bonoli, Giuliano. 2001. "Switzerland: Stubborn Institutions in a Changing Society." In *Welfare States under Pressure,* edited by Peter Taylor-Gooby, 123–46. Thousand Oaks, CA: Sage.

Bonoli, Giuliano, Vic George, and Peter Taylor-Gooby. 2000. *European Welfare Futures: Towards a Theory of Retrenchment.* Cambridge: Polity Press.

Boswell, Terry, and Christopher Chase-Dunn. 1999. *The Spiral of Capitalism and Socialism: Toward Global Democracy.* Boulder, CO: Lynne Rienner.

Bourdieu, Pierre. 1979. "Public Opinion Does Not Exist." In *Communication and Class Struggle: An Anthology in 2 Volumes.* Edited by Armand Mattelart and Seth Siegelaub, 124–30. New York: International General.

Bradley, David, Evelyne Huber, Stephanie Moller, François Nielsen, and John Stephens. 2003. "Distribution and Redistribution in Postindustrial Democracies." *World Politics* 55:193–228.

Brady, David. 2003a. "Rethinking the Sociological Measurement of Poverty." *Social Forces* 81:715–52.

———. 2003b. "The Politics of Poverty: Left Political Institutions, the Welfare State, and Poverty." *Social Forces* 82:557–88.

Brady, David, Jason Beckfield, and Martin Seeleib-Kaiser. 2005. "Economic Globalization and the Welfare State in Affluent Democracies, 1975–2001." *American Sociological Review* 70:921–48.

Briggs, Asa. 1961. "The Welfare State in Historical Perspective." *Archives Européennes de Sociologie* 2:221–58.

Brint, Steven, and Susan Kelley. 1993. "The Social Bases of Political Beliefs in the United States: Interests, Cultures, and Normative Pressures in Comparative-Historical Perspective." *Research in Political Sociology* 6:277–317.

Brooks, Clem. 2000. "Civil Rights Liberalism and the Suppression of a Republican Political Realignment in the U.S., 1972–1996." *American Sociological Review* 65:482–505.

———. 2002. "Religious Influence and the Politics of Family Decline Concern: Trends, Sources, and U.S. Political Behavior." *American Sociological Review* 67:191–211.

———. 2006. "Voters, Satisficing, and Policymaking: Recent Directions in the Study of Electoral Politics." *Annual Review of Sociology* 32:191–211.

Brooks, Clem, and David Brady. 1999. "Income, Economic Voting, and Long-Term Political Change in the U.S., 1952–1996." *Social Forces:* 77:1339–74.

Brooks, Clem, and Jeff Manza. 1997. "Class Politics and Political Change in the United States, 1952–1992." *Social Forces* 79:379–409.

———. 2006a. "Social Policy Responsiveness in Developed Democracies."*American Sociological Review* 71:474–94.

———. 2006b. "Why Do Welfare States Persist?"*Journal of Politics* 68: 816–27.

Brooks, Clem, Jeff Manza, and Catherine Bolzendahl. 2003. "Voting Behavior and Political Sociology: Theories, Debates, and Future Directions." *Research in Political Sociology* 12:137–73.

Brooks, Joel. 1987. "The Opinion-Policy Nexus in France: Do Institutions and Ideology Make a Difference?" *Journal of Politics* 49:465–80.

———. 1990. "The Opinion-Policy Nexus in Germany." *Public Opinion Quarterly* 54: 508–29.

Brown, Lester. 2003. *Plan B: Rescuing a Planet under Stress and a Civilization in Trouble.* New York: Norton.

Brown, Michael, ed. 1988. *Remaking the Welfare State: Retrenchment and Social Policy in America and Europe.* Philadelphia: Temple University Press.

Brubaker, Rogers. 1996. *Nationalism Reframed: Nationhood and the National Question in the New Europe.* Cambridge: Cambridge University Press.

Burns, Nancy, Kay Schlozman, and Sidney Verba. 2001. *The Private Roots of Public Action: Gender, Equality, and Political Participation.* Cambridge: Harvard University Press.

Burstein, Paul. 1991. "Policy Domains: Organization, Culture, and Policy Outcomes." *Annual Review of Sociology* 17:327–50.

———. 1998. "Bringing the Public Back In: Should Sociologists Consider the Impact of Public Opinion on Public Policy?" *Social Forces* 77:27–62.

———. 1999. "Social Movements and Public Policy."In *How Social Movements Matter.* Edited by Marco Giugni, Doug McAdam, and Charles Tilly, 3–21. Minneapolis: University of Minnesota Press.

———. 2003. "The Impact of Public Opinion on Public Policy: A Review and an Agenda." *Political Research Quarterly* 56:29–40.

———. 2006. "Why Estimates of the Impact of Public Opinion on Public Policy Are Too High: Empirical and Theoretical Implications." *Social Forces* 94:2273–89.

Campbell, Angus, Philip Converse, Warren Miller, and Donald Stokes. 1960. *The American Voter.* New York: Wiley.

Campbell, John. 2002. "Ideas, Politics, and Public Policy." *Annual Review of Sociology* 28:21–38.

Carmines, Edward, and Huckfeldt, Robert. 1996. "Political Behavior: An Overview." In *A New Handbook of Political Science.* Edited by Robert Goodin and Hans-Dieter Klingemann, 223–54 . New York: Oxford University Press.

Castles, Francis Geoffrey. 1994. "On Religion and Public Policy: Does Catholicism Make a Difference?" *European Journal of Political Research* 25:12–40.

————. 1995. "Welfare State Development in Southern Europe." *West European Politics* 18:291–313.

————. 1996. "Needs-Based Strategies of Social Protection in Australia and New Zealand." In *Welfare States in Transition: National Adaptations in Global Economies*. Edited by Gøsta Esping-Andersen, 88–115 Thousand Oaks, CA: Sage.

————. 2004. *The Future of the Welfare State: Crisis Myths and Crisis Realities*. New York: Oxford University Press.

Castles, Francis Geoffrey, and Peter Mair. 1984. "Left-Right Political Scales: Some 'Expert' Judgments." *European Journal of Political Research* 12:73–88.

Castles, Francis Geoffrey, and Deborah Mitchell. 1993. "Worlds of Welfare and Families of Nations." In *Families of Nations*. Edited by Francis Geoffrey, 93–128. Aldershot, UK: Dartmouth.

Center for Political Studies. 2003. *American National Election Studies*. 1976–2000 pre- and post-election surveys. Machine-readable data files and codebooks. Ann Arbor, MI: National Election Studies and Inter-university Consortium for Political and Social Research.

Conley, Dalton, and Kristen W. Springer. 2001. "Welfare State and Infant Mortality." *American Journal of Sociology* 107:768–807.

Converse, Philip E. 1964. "The Nature of Belief Systems in Mass Publics." In *Ideology and Discontent*. Edited by David Apter, 206–61. New York: Free Press.

Cook, Karen. 2000. "Advances in the Microfoundations of Sociology: Recent Developments and New Challenges for Social Psychology." *Contemporary Sociology* 29:685–92.

Coughlin, Richard. 1980. *Ideology, Public Opinion, & Welfare Policy*. Berkeley: Institute of International Studies, University of California.

Cutright, Phillips. 1965. "Political Structure, Economic Development, and National Social Security Programs." *American Journal of Sociology* 70:537–50.

————. 1967. "Income Redistribution. A Cross-National Analysis." *Social Forces* 46:180–89.

Crosland, Anthony. 1964. *The Future of Socialism*. Abridged and rev. ed. New York: Schocken Books.

Dalton, Russell. 1996. *Citizen Politics: Public Opinion and Political Parties in Advanced Industrial Democracies*. 2nd ed. Chatham: Chatham House.

David, Paul. 1985. "Clio and the Economics of QWERTY." *American Economic Review* 75: 332–37.

Davidson, Russell, and James MacKinnon. 1993. *Estimation and Inference in Econometrics*. New York: Oxford University Press.

Davis, James, Tom W. Smith, and Peter Marsden. 2000. *General Social Surveys, 1972–2000*. Machine-readable data files and codebook. Storrs: Roper Center for Public Opinion Research.

Delli Carpini, Michael X., and Scott Keeter. 1996. *What Americans Know about Politics and Why It Matters*. New Haven: Yale University Press.

Dinardo, John, and Thomas Lemieux. 1997. "Diverging Male Wage Inequality in the United States and Canada, 1981–1988: Do Institutions Explain the Difference?" *Industrial and Labour Relations Review* 50:629–51.

DiPrete, Thomas A. 2002. "Life Course Risks, Mobility Regimes, and Mobility Consequences: A Comparison of Sweden, Germany, and the United States." *American Journal of Sociology* 108:267–309.

DiPrete, Thomas A., and McManus, Patricia A. 2000. "Family Change, Employment Transitions, and the Welfare State: Household Income Dynamics in the United States and Germany." *American Sociological Review* 65:343–70.

Domhoff, G. William. 1998. *Who Rules America? Power and Politics in the Year 2000.* Mountain View, CA: Mayfield.

———. 2002. "The Power Elite, Public Policy, and Public Opinion." In *Navigating Public Opinion: Polls Policy and the Future of American Democracy.* Edited by Jeff Manza, Fay Lomax Cook, and Benjamin I. Page, 124–40. New York: Oxford University Press:

Downs, Anthony. 1957. *An Economic Theory of Democracy.* New York: Harper and Row.

Duch, Raymond, Harvey Palmer, and Christopher Anderson. 2000. "Heterogeneity in Perceptions of National Economic Conditions." *American Journal of Political Science* 44:635–52.

Ebbinghaus, Bernhard, and Jelle Visser. 2000. *The Societies of Europe: Trade Unions in Western Europe since 1945.* New York: Grove's Dictionaries.

Edlund, Jonas. 2003. "Attitudes toward Taxation: Ignorant and Incoherent?" *Scandinavian Political Studies* 26:145–67.

Eliasoph, Nina. 1998. *Avoiding Politics: How Americans Produce Apathy in Everyday Life.* New York: Cambridge University Press.

Elster, Jon. 1989. *Nuts and Bolts for the Social Sciences.* New York: Cambridge University Press.

Erie, Steven P., and Martin Rein. 1988. "Women and the Welfare State." In *The Politics of the Gender Gap.* Edited by Carol Mueller, 173–91. Newbury Park, CA: Sage.

Erikson, Robert, Michael MacKuen, and James Stimson. 2002a. *The Macro Polity.* New York: Cambridge University Press.

———. 2002b. "Public Opinion and Policy: Causal Flow in a Macro System Model." In *Navigating Public Opinion: Polls, Policy, and the Future of American Democracy.* Edited by Jeff Manza, Fay Lomax Cook, and Benjamin Page, 33–53. New York: Oxford University Press.

Erikson, Robert, and Kent Tedin. 1995. *American Public Opinion: Its Origins, Content, and Impact.* 5th ed. Boston: Allyn and Bacon.

Esping-Andersen, Gøsta. 1978. "Social Class, Social Democracy, and the State: Party Policy and Party Decomposition in Denmark and Sweden." *Comparative Politics* 11:42–58.

————. 1985. *Politics against Markets: The Social Democratic Road to Power.* Princeton, NJ: Princeton University Press.

————. 1990. *The Three Worlds of Welfare Capitalism.* Princeton, NJ: Princeton University Press.

————. 1996a. "After the Golden Age? Welfare State Dilemmas in a Global Economy." In *Welfare States in Transition: National Adaptations in Global Economies.* Edited by Gøsta Esping-Andersen, 1–31. Thousand Oaks, CA: Sage.

————. 1996b. "Positive-Sum Solutions in a World of Trade-Offs?" In *Welfare States in Transition: National Adaptations in Global Economies.* Edited by Gøsta Esping-Andersen, 256–67. Thousand Oaks, CA: Sage.

————. 2000. "The Sustainability of Welfare States into the Twenty-First Century." *International Journal of Health Services* 30:1–12.

Estevez-Abe, Margarita. 2002. "Negotiating Welfare Reforms: Actors and Institutions in the Japanese Welfare State." In *Restructuring the Welfare State: Political Institutions and Policy Change.* Edited by Bo Rothstein and Sven Steinmo, 157–83. New York: Palgrave Macmillan.

Evans, Peter, Dietrich Rueschemeyer, and Theda Skocpol (eds.). 1985. *Bringing the State Back In.* New York: Cambridge University Press.

Eyerman, Ron. 2004. "The Past in the Present: Culture and the Transmission of Memory." *Acta Sociologica* 47:159–69.

Ferrera, Maurizio. 1996. "A New Social Contract? The Four Social Europes: Between Universalism and Selectivity." EUI RSC 1996/36. San Domenico, Italy: European University Institute.

————. 1997. "The Uncertain Future of the Italian Welfare State." *West European Politics* 20:231–49.

Fine, Gary Alan. 2001. *Difficult Reputations: Collective Memories of the Evil, Inept, and Controversial.* Chicago: University of Chicago Press.

Fiorina, Morris. 1981. *Retrospective Voting in American National Elections.* New Haven: Yale University Press.

Firebaugh, Glenn. 1997. *Analyzing Repeated Surveys.* Thousand Oaks, CA: Sage.

Flora, Peter, and Jens Alber. 1981. "Modernization, Democratization, and the Development of Welfare States in Western Europe." In *The Development of Welfare States in Europe and America.* Edited by Peter Flora and Arnold J. Heidenheimer, 37–80. New Brunswick, NJ: Transaction Press.

Form, William. 1979. "Comparative Industrial Sociology and the Convergence Hypothesis." *Annual Review of Sociology* 5:1–25.

Fukuyama, Francis. 1992. *The End of History and the Last Man.* New York: Avon Books.

Galbraith, John K. 1985[1971]. *The New Industrial State.* New York: Houghton Mifflin.

Gangl, Markus. 2004. "Welfare States and the Scar Effects of Unemployment: A

Comparative Analysis of the United States and West Germany." *American Journal of Sociology* 109:1319–64.

Ganzeboom, Harry, Donald Treiman, and Wout Ultee. 1991. "Comparative Intergenerational Stratification Research: Three Generations and Beyond." *Annual Review of Sociology* 17:277–302.

Garrett, Geoffrey. 1998. *Partisan Politics in the Global Economy.* New York: Cambridge University Press.

Geer, John. 1996. *From Tea Leaves to Opinion Polls: A Theory of Democratic Leadership.* New York: Columbia University Press.

Gilbert, Neil. 2002. *Transformation of the Welfare State: The Silent Surrender of Public Responsibility.* New York: Oxford University Press.

Gilens, Martin. 1999. *Why Americans Hate Welfare.* Chicago: University of Chicago Press.

Gillis, John, ed. 1996. *Commemorations: The Politics of National Identity.* Princeton, NJ: Princeton University Press.

Ginsberg, Benjamin. 1986. *The Captive Public.* New York: Basic Books.

Ginsburg, Norman. 2001. "Globalization and the Liberal Welfare States." In *Globalization and European Welfare States: Challenges and Change.* Edited by Robert Sykes, Bruno Palier, and Pauline Prior, 173–91. Basingstoke, UK: Palgrave.

Granovetter, Mark. 1985. "Economic Action and Social Structure: The Problem of Embeddedness." *American Journal of Sociology* 91:481–510.

———. 1995. *Getting a Job.* 2nd ed. Chicago: University of Chicago Press.

———. 2005. "The Impact of Social Structure on Economic Outcomes." *Journal of Economic Perspectives* 19:33–50.

Green, Donald, and Ian Shapiro. 1994. *Pathologies of Rational Choice Theory: A Critique of Applications in Political Science.* New Haven: Yale University Press.

Greene, William. 2000. *Econometric Analysis.* 4th ed. Upper Saddle River, NJ: Prentice Hall.

Greve, Bent. 1996. "Indications of Social Policy Convergence in Europe." *Social Policy & Administration* 30:348–67.

Grusky, David B., ed. 2001. *Social Stratification: Class, Race, and Gender in Comparative Perspective.* 2nd ed. Boulder, CO: Westview Press.

Guest, Dennis. 1991[1980]. *The Emergence of Social Security in Canada.* Vancouver: University of British Columbia Press.

Guillen, Mauro F., Randall Collins, Paula England, and Marshall Meyer, eds. 2002. *The New Economic Sociology: Developments in an Emerging Field.* New York: Russell Sage Foundation.

Hacker, Jacob. 2002. *The Divided Welfare State.* New York: Cambridge University Press.

Hacker, Jacob, and Paul Pierson. 2005. "Abandoning the Middle: The Bush Tax Cuts and the Limits of Democratic Control." *Perspectives on Politics* 3:15–31.

Hall, Peter, and David Soskice, eds. 2001. *Varieties of Capitalism: The Institutional Foundations of Comparative Advantage*. New York: Oxford University Press.

Hall, Peter, and Rosemary Taylor. 1996. "Political Science and the Three New Institutionalisms." *Political Studies* 44:936–57.

Hausman, Jerry. 1978. "Specification Tests in Econometrics." *Econometrica* 46:1251–70.

———. 1983. "Specification and Estimation of Simultaneous Equations Models." In *Handbook of Econometrics*. Edited by Zvi Griliches and Michael Intriligator, 391–448. Amsterdam: North-Holland.

Hawthorne, Geoffrey. 1991. *Plausible Worlds: Possibility and Understanding in History and the Social Sciences*. New York: Cambridge University Press.

Hayek, Friedrich A. 1994[1944]. *The Road to Serfdom*. Chicago: University of Chicago Press.

Heath, Anthony, Roger Jowell, John Curtice, Geoffrey Evans, J. Field, and Sharon Witherspoon. 1991. *Understanding Political Change: The British Voter, 1964–1987*. London: Pergamon Press.

Heclo, Hugh. 1974. *The Private Government of Public Money: Community and Policy inside British Politics*. Berkeley: University of California Press.

Herbst, Susan. 1993. *Numbered Voices: How Opinion Polling Has Shaped American Politics*. Chicago: University of Chicago Press.

———. 1998. *Reading Public Opinion: Political Actors View the Democratic Process*. Chicago: University of Chicago Press.

Hicks, Alexander. 1999. *Social Democracy and Welfare Capitalism: A Century of Income Security Politics*. Ithaca, NY: Cornell University Press.

Hill, Kim Q., Jan E. Leighley, and Angela Hinton-Andersson. 1995. "Lower-Class Policy Mobilization and Policy Linkage in the United States." *American Journal of Political Science* 39:75–86.

Homans, George. 1964. "Bringing Men Back In." *American Sociological Review* 29:809–18.

Hsiao, Cheng. 1986. *Analysis of Panel Data*. New York: Cambridge University Press.

Huber, Evelyne, Charles Ragin, and John D. Stephens. 1993. "Social Democracy, Christian Democracy, Constitutional Structure, and the Welfare State." *American Journal of Sociology* 99:711–49.

Huber, Evelyne, Charles Ragin, John D. Stephens, David Brady, and Jason Beckfield. 2004. *Comparative Welfare States Dataset*. Machine-readable data files and codebooks. Chapel Hill: Department of Political Science, University of North Carolina.

Huber, Evelyne, and John Stephens. 2000. "Partisan Governance, Women's Employment, and the Social Democratic Service State." *American Sociological Review* 65:323–42.

———. 2001. *Development and Crisis of the Welfare State: Parties and Policies in Global Markets*. Chicago: University of Chicago Press.

Immergut, Ellen. 1992. *The Political Construction of Interests: National Health Insurance Politics in Switzerland, France, and Sweden, 1930–1970*. New York: Cambridge University Press.

———. 1998. "The Theoretical Core of the New Institutionalism." *Politics & Society* 26:5–34.

International Monetary Fund. 2003. *Balance of Payments Statistics Yearbook*. Washington, DC: IMF.

International Social Survey Program. 1988. *Role of Government I, 1985–1986*. Machine-readable data files and codebooks. Ann Arbor, MI: Inter-University Consortium for Political and Social Research.

———. 1993. *Role of Government II, 1990*. Machine-readable data files and codebooks. Ann Arbor, MI: Inter-University Consortium for Political and Social Research.

———. 1994. *Religion I, 1991*. Machine-readable data files and codebooks. Ann Arbor, MI: Inter-University Consortium for Political and Social Research.

———. 1999. *Role of Government III, 1996*. Machine-readable data files and codebooks. Ann Arbor, MI: Inter-University Consortium for Political and Social Research.

———. 2001. *Religion II, 1998*. Machine-readable data files and codebooks. Ann Arbor, MI: Inter-University Consortium for Political and Social Research.

Iversen, Torben. 2001. "The Dynamics of Welfare State Expansion: Trade Openness, De-Industrialization, and Partisan Politics." In *The New Politics of the Welfare State*. Edited by Paul Pierson, 45–79. New York: Oxford University Press.

Iversen, Torben, and Thomas Cusack. 2000. "The Causes of Welfare State Expansion: Deindustrialization or Globalization?" *World Politics* 52:313–49.

Iversen, Torben, and David Soskice. 2001. "An Asset Theory of Social Policy Preferences." *American Political Science Review* 95:875–93.

Jacobs, Lawrence. 1993. *The Health of Nations*. Ithaca, NY: Cornell University Press.

Jacobs, Lawrence, and Robert Shapiro. 2000. *Politicians Don't Pander: Political Manipulation and the Loss of Democratic Responsiveness*. Chicago: University of Chicago Press.

Kahneman, Daniel, Paul Slovic, and Amos Tversky. 1982. *Judgment under Uncertainty: Heuristics and Biases*. New York: Cambridge University Press.

Kangas, Olli. 1994. "The Merging of Welfare State Models? Past and Present Trends in Finnish and Swedish Social Policy." *Journal of European Social Policy* 4:79–94.

Katzenstein, Peter. 1985. *Small States in World Markets*. Ithaca, NY: Cornell University Press.

———. 2003. "*Small States* and Small States Revisited." *New Political Economy* 8:9–11, 18–19.

Kautto, Mikko, Johan Fritzell, Bjorn Hvinden, Jon Kvist, and Hannu Uusitalo. 2001a. "Introduction: How Distinct Are the Nordic Welfare States?" In *Nordic Welfare States in the European Context.* Edited by Mikko Kautto, Johan Fritzell, Bjorn Hvinden, Jon Kvist, and Hannu Uusitalo, 1–17. New York: Routledge.

———. 2001b. *Nordic Welfare States in the European Context.* New York: Routledge.

Kenworthy, Lane. 1999. "Do Social-Welfare Policies Reduce Poverty? A Cross-National Assessment." *Social Forces* 77:1119–39.

Kerr, Clark, John Dunlop, Friederich Harbinson, and Charles Myers. 1960. *Industrialism and Industrial Man.* Cambridge: Harvard University Press.

Kersbergen, Kees van. 1999. "Contemporary Christian Democracy and the Demise of the Politics of Mediation." In *Continuity and Change in Contemporary Capitalism.* Edited by Herbert Kitschelt, Peter Lange, Gary Marks, and John Stephens, 346–70. New York: Cambridge University Press.

Kiewiet, Roderick. 1983. *Macroeconomics and Micropolitics: The Electoral Effects of Economic Issues.* Chicago: University of Chicago Press.

Kinder, Donald, and Lynn Sanders. 1996. *Divided by Color.* Chicago: University of Chicago Press.

Kingdon, John. 1981. *Congressmen's Voting Decisions.* 2nd ed. New York: Harper and Row.

Kiser, Edgar. 1999. "Comparing Varieties of Agency Theory in Economics, Political Science, and Sociology: An Illustration from State Policy Implementation." *Sociological Theory* 17:146–70.

Kiser, Edgar and Margaret Levi. 1996. "Using Counterfactuals in Historical Analysis: Theories of Revolution." In *Counterfactual Thought Experiments in World Politics: Logical, Methodological, and Psychological Perspectives,* edited by Philip Tetlock and Aaron Belkin, 187–207. Princeton, NJ: Princeton University Press.

Kitschelt, Herbert. 1999. "European Social Democracy: Between Political Economy and Electoral Competition." In *Continuity and Change in Contemporary Capitalism.* Edited by Herbert Kitschelt, Peter Lange, Gary Marks, and John D. Stephens, 317–45. New York: Cambridge University Press.

Kluegel, James, and Masaru Miyano. 1995. "Justice Beliefs and Support for the Welfare State in Advanced Capitalism." In *Social Justice and Political Change: Public Opinion in Capitalist and Post-Communist States.* Edited by James Kluegel, David Mason, and Bernd Wegener, 81–105 . New York: Aldine de Gruyter.

Knoke, David, Franz Urban Pappi, Jeffrey Broadbent, and Yutaka Tsujinaka. 1996. *Comparing Policy Networks: Labor Politics in the U.S., Germany, and Japan.* New York: Cambridge University Press.

Knutsen, Oddbjorn. 1995. "Party Choice." In *The Impact of Values.* Edited by Jan van Deth and Elinor Scarbrough, 460–503. New York: Oxford University Press.

Kornhauser, William. 1959. *The Politics of Mass Society.* New York: Free Press.

Korpi, Walter. 1983. *The Democratic Class Struggle*. London: Routledge and Kegan Paul.

———. 1989. "Power, Politics, and State Autonomy in the Development of Social Citizenship: Social Rights during Sickness in Eighteen OECD Countries since 1930." *American Sociological Review* 54:309–28.

———. 2000. "Faces of Inequality: Gender, Class, and Patterns of Inequalities in Different Types of Welfare States." *Social Politics* 7:127–91.

———. 2003. "Welfare-State Regress in Western Europe: Politics, Institutions, Globalization, and Europeanization." *Annual Review of Sociology* 29:589–609.

———. 2004. *Open Letter to Research Committee 19 of the International Sociological Association*. Stockholm: Swedish Institute for Social Research.

Korpi, Walter, and Joakim Palme. 1998. "The Paradox of Redistribution and Strategies of Equality: Welfare State Institutions, Inequality, and Poverty in the Western Countries." *American Sociological Review* 63:661–87.

———. 2003. "New Politics and Class Politics in the Context of Austerity and Globalization: Welfare State Regress in 18 Countries, 1975–95." *American Political Science Review* 97:425–46.

Kosenen, Pekka. 1995. "European Welfare State Models: Converging Trends." *International Journal of Sociology* 25:81–110.

Kramer, Gerald. 1983. "The Ecological Fallacy Revisited: Aggregate- versus Individual-Level Findings on Economics and Elections, and Sociotropic Voting." *American Political Science Review* 77: 92–111.

Kuhnle, Stein, and Matti Alestalo. 2000. "Introduction: Growth, Adjustments and Survival of European Welfare States." In *Survival of the European Welfare State*. Edited by Stein Kuhnle, 3–18. London: Routledge.

Lane, Robert. 1962. *Political Ideology: Why the American Common Man Believes What He Does*. New York: Free Press.

Lapinski, John S., Charles R. Riemann, Robert Y. Shapiro, Matthew F. Stevens, and Lawrence R. Jacobs. 1998. "Welfare State Regimes and Subjective Well-Being: A Cross-National Study." *International Journal of Public Opinion Research* 10:2–24.

Larsen, Christian. 2006. *The Institutional Logic of Welfare Attitudes: How Welfare Regimes Influence Public Support*. Aldershot, UK: Ashgate Publishing Ltd.

Lewis, Justin. 2001. *Constructing Public Opinion: How Political Elites Do What They Like and Why We Seem to Go Along with It*. New York: Columbia University Press.

Lewis-Beck, Michael, and Mary Stegmaier. 2000. "Economic Determinants of Electoral Outcomes." *Annual Review of Political Science* 3:183–219.

Lieberman, Robert. 1998. *Shifting the Color Line: Race and the American Welfare State*. Cambridge: Harvard University Press.

Lijphart, Arend. 1994. "Democracies: Forms, Performance, and Constitutional Engineering." *European Journal of Political Research* 25:1–17.

————. 1999. *Patterns of Democracy: Government Forms and Performance in Thirty-Six Countries*. New Haven: Yale University Press.

Lindbom, Anders. 2001. "Dismantling the Social Democratic Welfare Model? Has the Swedish Welfare State Lost Its Defining Characteristics?" *Scandinavian Political Studies* 24:171–93.

Lipset, Seymour Martin. 1963. *The First New Nation: The United States in Historical and Comparative Perspective*. New York: Basic Books.

————. 1981. *Political Man: The Social Bases of Politics*. Expanded ed. Baltimore: Johns Hopkins University Press.

————. 1996. *American Exceptionalism: A Double-Edged Sword*. New York: Norton.

Lipset, Seymour Martin, and Stein Rokkan. 1967. *Party Systems and Voter Alignments: Cross-National Perspectives*. New York: Free Press.

Long, Scott, and Laurie Ervin. 2000. "Using Heteroscedasticity Consistent Standard Errors in the Linear Regression Model." *American Statistician* 54:217–24.

Lupia, Arthur, Mathew McCubbins, and Samuel Popkin, eds. 2000. *Elements of Reason: Cognition, Choice, and the Bounds of Rationality*. New York: Cambridge University Press.

Manza, Jeff, and Clem Brooks. 1999. *Social Cleavages and Political Change: Voter Alignments and U.S. Party Coalitions*. New York: Oxford University Press.

Manza, Jeff, and Fay Lomax Cook. 2002. "A Democratic Polity? Three Views of Policy Responsiveness in the United States." *American Politics Quarterly* 30: 630–67.

Manza, Jeff, Fay Lomax Cook, and Benjamin Page, eds. 2002. *Navigating Public Opinion: Polls, Policy, and the Future of American Democracy*. New York: Oxford University Press.

Marcuse, Herbert. 1964. *One-Dimensional Man: Studies in the Ideology of Advanced Industrial Society*. Boston: Beacon Press.

Marklund, Stefan. 1988. *Paradise Lost?* Lund: Arkiv.

Marshall, T. H. 1950. *Citizenship and Social Class*. New York: Cambridge University Press.

Martinussen, Willy. 1993. "Welfare-State Support in Achievement-Oriented Hearts: The Case of Norway." In *Welfare Trends in the Scandinavian Countries*. Edited by Erik Hansen, Stein Ringen, Hannu Uusitalo, and Robert Erikson, 49–60. Armonk, NY: M. E. Sharpe.

McAdam, Doug, and Yang Su. 2002. "The War at Home: Antiwar Protests and Congressional Voting, 1965 to 1973." *American Sociological Review* 67:696–721.

McClosky, Herbert, and Alida Brill. 1983. *Dimensions of Tolerance: What Americans Believe about Civil Liberties*. New York: Russell Sage.

McClosky, Herbert, and John Zaller. 1984. *The American Ethos: Public Attitudes toward Capitalism and Democracy*. Cambridge: Harvard University Press.

McFate, Kathryn, Roger Lawson, and William Julius Wilson (eds.). 1995. *Poverty, Inequality, and the Future of Social Policy: Western States in the New World Order.* New York: Russell Sage Foundation.

McManus, Patricia, and Thomas DiPrete. 2001. "Losers and Winners: The Financial Consequences of Separation and Divorce for Men." *American Sociological Review* 66:246–68.

Mead, Lawrence. 1986. *Beyond Entitlement: The Social Obligations of Citizenship.* New York: Free Press.

Mehrtens, John. 2004. "Three Worlds of Public Opinion: Values, Variation, and the Effect on Social Policy." *International Journal of Public Opinion Research* 16:115–43.

Meyer, John, John Boli, George Thomas, and Francisco Ramirez. 1997. "World Society and the Nation-State." *American Journal of Sociology* 103:144–81.

Meyer, John, John Boli-Bennett, and Christopher Chase-Dunn. 1975. "Convergence and Divergence in Development." *Annual Review of Sociology* 1:223–46.

Meyer, John, and Brian Rowan. 1977. "Institutionalized Organizations: Formal Structure as Myth and Ceremony." *American Journal of Sociology* 83:340–63.

Misra, Ramesh. 1999. *Globalization and the Welfare State.* Cheltenham and Northampton, UK: Edward Elger.

Misra, Joya, and Alexander Hicks. 1994. "Catholicism and Unionization in Affluent Postwar Democracies: Catholicism, Culture, Party, and Unionization." *American Sociological Review* 59:304–26.

Moller, Stephanie, David Bradley, Evelyne Huber, François Nielsen, and John Stephens. 2003. "Determinants of Relative Poverty in Advanced Capitalist Democracies." *American Sociological Review* 68:22–51.

Monroe, Alan. 1998. "Public Opinion and Public Policy, 1980–1993." *Public Opinion Quarterly* 62:6–28.

Montanari, Ingalill. 2001. "Modernization, Globalization and the Welfare State: A Comparative Analysis of Old and New Convergence of Social Insurance since 1930." *British Journal of Sociology* 52:469–94.

Murray, Charles. 1994[1984]. *Losing Ground: American Social Policy, 1950–1980.* New York: Basic Books.

Mutz, Diana. 2006. *Hearing the Other Side: Deliberative versus Participatory Democracy.* New York: Cambridge University Press.

Myles, John. 1984. *Old Age in the Welfare State: The Political Economy of Public Pensions.* Boston: Little, Brown.

———. 2006. "Comment on Brooks and Manza: Welfare States and Public Opinion." *American Sociological Review* 71:495–98.

Niemi, Richard, and Herbert Weisberg. 2001. *Controversies in Voting Behavior.* 4th ed. Washington DC: Congressional Quarterly Press.

Nozick, Robert. 1974. *Anarchy, State, and Utopia.* New York: Basic Books.

Nunn, Clyde Z., Harry J. Crockett Jr., and J. Allen Williams Jr. 1978. *Tolerance for Nonconformity: A National Survey of Americans' Changing Commitment to Civil Liberties.* San Francisco: Jossey-Bass.

O'Connor, James. 1973. *The Fiscal Crisis of the State.* London: Palgrave Macmillan.

O'Connor, Julia, Ann Orloff, and Sheila Shaver. 1999. *States, Markets, Families: Gender, Liberalism, and Social Policy in Australia, Canada, Great Britain, and the United States.* New York: Cambridge University Press.

Ohmae, Kenichi. 1996. *The End of the Nation State: The Rise of Regional Economies.* New York: Free Press.

Olick, Jeffrey. 1999a. "Collective Memory: The Two Cultures." *Sociological Theory* 17: 333–48.

———. 2003. *States of Memory: Continuities, Conflicts, and Transformations in National Retrospection.* Durham, NC: Duke University Press.

Organization for Economic Cooperation and Development. 2002a. *Health Data.* http://www.sourceoecd.org.

———. 2002b. *Social Expenditures Database* (SOCX). http://www.sourceoecd .org.

———. 2003a. *Labour Force Statistics* [various years]. http://www.oecd.org.

———. 2003b. *Main Economic Indicators* [various years]. http://www.oecd.org.

———. 2003c. *Historical Statistics* [various years]. http://www.oecd.org.

———. 2003d. *National Accounts* [various years]. http://www.oecd.org.

———. 2005. *Social Expenditures Database* [1980–2001]. http://www.sourceoecd .org.

Orloff, Ann. 1993a. "Gender and the Social Rights of Citizenship: The Comparative Analysis of Gender Relations and Welfare States." *American Sociological Review* 58:303–28.

———. 1993b. *The Politics of Pensions: A Comparative Analysis of Britain, Canada, and the United States, 1880–1940.* Madison: University of Wisconsin Press.

———. 1993c. "The Role of State Formation and State Building in Social Policy Developments: The Politics of Pensions in Britain, the United States and Canada, 1880s–1930s." *Political Power and Social Theory* 8:3–44.

Page, Benjamin. 2002. "The Semi-Sovereign Public." In *Navigating Public Opinion: Polls, Policy, and the Future of American Democracy.* Edited by Jeff Manza, Fay Lomax Cook, and Benjamin Page, 325–344. New York: Oxford University Press.

Page, Benjamin, and Robert Shapiro. 1983. "Effects of Public Opinion on Policy." *American Political Science Review* 77:175–90.

———. 1992. *The Rational Public: Fifty Years of Trends in Americans' Policy Preferences.* Chicago: University of Chicago Press.

Page, Benjamin, and James R. Simmons. 2000. *What Government Can Do: Dealing with Poverty and Inequality.* Chicago: University of Chicago Press.

Palier, Bruno. 2001. "Reshaping the Social Policy-Making Framework in France." In *Welfare States under Pressure*. Edited by Peter Taylor-Gooby, 52–74. Thousand Oaks, CA: Sage.

Pampel, Fred, and John Williamson. 1985. "Age Structure, Politics, and Cross-National Patterns of Public Pension Expenditures." *American Sociological Review* 50:782–99.

———. 1988. "Welfare Spending in Advanced Industrial Democracies, 1950–1980." *American Journal of Sociology* 93:1424–56.

Parkin, Frank. 1971. *Class Inequality and Political Order*. New York: Praeger.

Parsons, Talcott. 1960. *Structure and Process in Modern Societies*. Glencoe, IL: Free Press.

———. 1971. *The System of Modern Societies*. Englewood Cliffs, NJ: Prentice-Hall.

Paxton, Pamela, and Sheri Kunovich. 2003. "Women's Political Representation: The Importance of Ideology." *Social Forces* 82:87–114.

Pettersen, Per Arnt. 1995. "The Welfare State: The Security Dimension." In *The Scope of Government*. Ole Borre and Elinor Scarbrough, 198–233. New York: Oxford University Press.

Petry, François. 1999. "The Opinion-Policy Relationship in Canada." *Journal of Politics* 61:540–50.

Pierson, Paul. 1993. " When Effect Becomes Cause: Policy Feedback and Political Change." *World Politics* 45:595–628.

———. 1994. *Dismantling the Welfare State? Reagan, Thatcher, and the Politics of Retrenchment*. New York: Cambridge University Press.

———. 1996. "The New Politics of the Welfare State." *World Politics* 48:143–79.

———. 2000. "Not Just What, but When: Timing and Sequence in Political Processes." *Studies in American Political Development* 14:72–92.

———. 2001a. "Coping with Permanent Austerity: Welfare State Restructuring in Affluent Democracies." In *The New Politics of the Welfare State*. Edited by Paul Pierson, 428–31. Oxford: Oxford University Press.

———. 2001b. "Investigating the Welfare State at Century's End." In *The New Politics of the Welfare State*. Edited by Paul Pierson, 1–14. New York: Oxford University Press.

Piven, Frances Fox (ed.). 1992. *Labor Parties in Postindustrial Societies*. New York: Oxford University Press.

Piven, Frances Fox, and Richard A. Cloward. 1971. *Regulating the Poor: The Functions of Public Welfare*. New York: Vintage Books.

———. 1997. "We Should Have Made a Plan!" *Politics & Society* 25:525–32.

Plumper, Thomas, Vera Troeger, and Philip Manow. 2005. "Panel Data Analysis in Comparative Politics: Linking Method to Theory." *European Journal of Political Research* 44:327–354.

Popkin, Samuel. 1991. *The Reasoning Voter: Communication and Persuasion in Presidential Campaigns*. Chicago: University of Chicago Press.

Porter, Kathryn, Kathy Larin, and Wendell Primus. 1999. *Social Security and Poverty among the Elderly: A National and State Perspective.* Washington, DC: Center on Budget and Policy Priorities.

Powell, G. Bingham Jr. 2000. *Elections as Instruments of Democracy.* New Haven: Yale University Press.

Przeworski, Adam. 1985. *Capitalism and Social Democracy.* New York: Cambridge University Press.

Quadagno, Jill. 1994. *The Color of Welfare: How Racism Undermined the War on Poverty.* New York: Oxford University Press.

Raftery, Adrian. 1995. "Bayesian Model Selection in Sociology." *Sociological Methodology* 25:111–63.

Rhodes, Mark. 1996. "Globalization and West European Welfare States: A Critical Review of Recent Debates." *Journal of European Social Policy* 6: 305–27.

Rifkin, Jeremy. 2004. *The European Dream: How Europe's Vision of the Future Is Quietly Eclipsing the American Dream.* New York: Putnam.

Rimlinger, Gaston. 1961. "Social Security, Incentives, and Controls in the U.S. and U.S.S.R." *Comparative Studies in Society and History* 4:104–24.

———. 1971. *Welfare Policy and Industrialization in Europe, America, and Russia.* New York: Wiley.

Ringen, Stein, and Hannu Uusitalo. 1992. "Income Distribution and Redistribution in the Nordic Welfare States." In *The Study of Welfare State Regimes.* Edited by Jon Eivind Kolberg, 69–91. 1992. New York: M. E. Sharpe.

Robinson, William. 1950. "Ecological Correlations and the Behavior of Individuals." *American Sociological Review* 15:351–57.

Rodrik, Dani. 1997. *Has Globalization Gone Too Far?* Washington, DC: Institute for International Economics.

Rogers, William. 1993. "sg17: Regression Standard Errors in Clustered Samples." *Stata Technical Bulletin* 13:19–23.

Rostow, Walt Whitman. 1960. *The Stages of Economic Growth: A Non-Communist Manifesto.* New York: Cambridge University Press.

Rothstein, Bo. 1998. *Just Institutions Matter: The Moral and Political Logic of the Universal Welfare State.* New York: Cambridge University Press.

Rothstein, Bo, and Sven Steinmo. 2002. "Restructuring Politics: Institutional Analysis and the Challenges of Modern Welfare States." In *Restructuring the Welfare State: Political Institutions and Policy Change.* Edited by Bo Rothstein and Sven Steinmo, 1–19. New York: Palgrave Macmillan.

Rueschemeyer, Dietrich, and Theda Skocpol (eds.). 1996. *States, Social Knowledge, and the Origins of Modern Social Policies.* Princeton, NJ: Princeton University Press.

Samuelson, Robert J. 1997. *Good Life and Its Discontents: The American Dream in the Age of Entitlement.* New York: Knopf.

Scharpf, Fritz. 1997. "Economic Integration, Democracy, and the Welfare State." *Journal of European Public Policy* 4:18–36.

Schudson, Michael. 1992. *Watergate in American Memory: How We Remember, Forget, and Reconstruct the Past*. New York: Basic Books.

Schwartz, Barry. 2000. *Abraham Lincoln and the Forge of National Memory*. Chicago: University of Chicago Press.

Schwartz, Barry, and Howard Schuman. 2005. "History, Commemoration, and Belief: Abraham Lincoln in American Memory, 1945–2001." *American Sociological Review* 70:183–203.

Schwartz, Herman. 1994. "Small States in Big Trouble: State Reorganization in Australia, Denmark, New Zealand, and Sweden in the 1980s." *World Politics* 46:527–55.

Scruggs, Lyle. 2004. *Welfare State Entitlements: A Comparative Institutional Analysis of Eighteen Welfare States, Version 1.0b*. Storrs: Department of Political Science, University of Connecticut.

Scruggs, Lyle, and James Allan. 2005. "Welfare State Decommodification in 18 OECD Countries: A Replication and Revision." Unpublished manuscript. Department of Political Science, University of Connecticut.

Shapiro, Robert. 1998. "Public Opinion, Elites, and Democracy." *Critical Review* 12:501–28.

Shapiro, Robert, and John Young. 1989. "Public Opinion and the Welfare State: The United States in Comparative Perspective." *Political Science Quarterly* 104:59–89.

Sherkat, Darren, and Christopher Ellison. 1997. "The Cognitive Structure of a Moral Crusade: Conservative Protestantism and Opposition to Pornography." *Social Forces* 75:957–82.

————. 1999. "Recent Developments and Current Controversies in the Sociology of Religion." *Annual Review of Sociology* 25:363–94.

Simon, Herbert. 1997. *Administrative Behavior: A Study of Decision-Making Processes in Administrative Organizations*. 4th ed. New York: Free Press.

Skrentny, John. 1996. *The Ironies of Affirmative Action: Politics, Culture, and Justice in America*. Chicago: University of Chicago Press.

Skocpol, Theda . 1992. *Protecting Soldiers and Mothers: The Political Origins of Social Policy in the United States*. Cambridge: Harvard University Press.

————. 1995. "Institutions and Institutionalism." *Polity* 28:83–140.

Smith, Christian. 1998. *American Evangelicalism: Embattled and Thriving*. Chicago: University of Chicago Press.

Smith, Tom W. 1987. "The Polls—A Report: The Welfare State in Cross-National Perspective." *Public Opinion Quarterly* 51:404–21.

————. 1990a. "Liberal and Conservative Trends in the United States since World War II." *Public Opinion Quarterly* 54:479–507.

————. 1990b. "Social Inequality in Cross-National Perspective." In *Attitudes to Inequality and the Role of Government*. Edited by J. W. Becker, James A. Davis, Peter Ester, and Peter P. Mohler, 21–31. Rijswijk, The Netherlands: Social and Cultural Planning Office.

Sniderman, Paul, Henry Brody, and Philip Tetlock. 1991. *Reasoning and Choice: Explorations in Political Psychology.* New York: Cambridge University Press.

Soroka, Stuart, and Christopher Wlezien. 2004. "Opinion Representation and Policy Feedback: Canada in Comparative Perspective." *Canadian Journal of Political Science* 37:531–59.

———. 2005. "Opinion-Policy Dynamics: Public Preferences and Public Expenditure in the United Kingdom." *British Journal of Political Science* 35: 665–89.

Standing, Guy. 1999. *Global Labour Flexibility: Seeking Distributive Justice.* London: Macmillan.

Statistics Norway. 2003. *Norwegian National Election Studies 1973–1997.* Machine-readable data files and codebooks. Oslo: Norwegian Election Research Program/Institute for Social Research.

Steensland, Brian, Jerry Park, Mark Regnerus, Lynn Robinson, Bradford Wilcox, and Robert Woodberry. 2000. "The Measure of American Religion: Toward Improving the State of the Art." *Social Forces* 79:291–318.

Steinmo, Sven. 1994. "American Exceptionalism Reconsidered: Culture or Institutions?" In *The Dynamics of American Politics.* Edited by Lawrence Dodd and Calvin Jillson, 106–31. Boulder, CO: Westview Press.

Stephens, John. 1979. *The Transition from Capitalism to Socialism.* London: Macmillan.

———. 1996. "The Scandinavian Welfare States: Achievements, Crisis, and Prospects." In *Welfare States in Transition: National Adaptations in Global Economies.* Edited by Gøsta Esping-Andersen, 32–65. Thousand Oaks, CA: Sage.

———. 2004. *Tides of Consent: How Public Opinion Shapes American Politics.* New York: Cambridge University Press.

Stimson, James A. 1991. *Public Opinion in America: Moods, Cycles, and Swings.* San Francisco: Westview Press.

Stimson, James A., Michael B. MacKuen, and Robert S. Erikson. 1995. "Dynamic Representation." *American Political Science Review* 89:543–65.

Stoker, Laura. 1992. "Interests and Ethics in Politics." *American Political Science Review* 86:369–80.

Stouffer, Samuel. 1992[1955]. *Communism, Conformity, and Civil Liberties.* New Brunswick, NJ: Transaction Publishers.

Sullivan, John L., James Piereson, and George E. Marcus. 1982. *Political Tolerance and American Democracy.* Chicago: University of Chicago Press.

Svallfors, Stefan. 1995. "The End of Class Politics? Structural Cleavages and Attitudes to Swedish Welfare Policies." *Acta Sociologica* 38:53–74.

———. 1997. "Worlds of Welfare and Attitudes to Redistribution: A Comparison of Eight Western Nations." *European Sociological Review* 13: 283–304.

———. 1999. "The Middle Class and Welfare State Retrenchment: Attitudes to Swedish Welfare Policies." In *The End of the Welfare State? Responses to State Retrenchment.* Edited by Stefan Svallfors and Peter Taylor-Gooby, 34–51. London and New York: Routledge.

Swank, Duane. 2002. *Global Capital, Political Institutions, and Policy Change in Developed Welfare States*. New York: Cambridge University Press.

Swedish Social Science Data Service. 2002. *Swedish Election Studies 1956–1999*. Machine-readable data files and codebooks. Göteborg: Swedish Social Science Data Service.

Taylor-Gooby, Peter. 1993. "What Citizens Want from the State." In *International Social Attitudes: The 10th BSA Report*. Edited by Roger Jowell, Lindsay Brook, and Lizanne Dowds, 82–101. Brookfield, VT: Dartmouth Publishing.

———. 1999. "'Hollowing Out' versus the New Interventionism." In *The End of the Welfare State? Responses to State Retrenchment*. Edited by Stefan Svallfors and Peter Taylor-Gooby, 1–12. London and New York: Routledge.

———. 2001. "Polity, Policy-Making and Welfare Futures." In *Welfare States under Pressure*. Edited by Peter Taylor-Gooby, 171–88. Thousand Oaks, CA: Sage.

Tetlock, Philip, and Aaron Belkin (eds.). 1996. *Counterfactual Thought Experiments in World Politics: Logical, Methodological, and Psychological Perspectives*. Princeton, NJ: Princeton University Press.

Thelen, Kathleen. 1999. "Historical Institutionalism in Comparative Politics." *Annual Review of Political Science* 2:369–404.

Therborn, Göran, Anders Kjellberg, Staffan Marklund, and Ulf Öhlund. 1978. "Sweden before and after Social Democracy: A First Overview." *Acta Sociologica* 1978 (supp.): 37–58.

Timonen, Virpi. 2001. "Earning Welfare Citizenship: Welfare State Reform in Finland and Sweden." In *Welfare States under Pressure*. Edited by Peter Taylor-Gooby, 29–51. Thousand Oaks, CA: Sage.

Titmuss, Richard. 1968. *Commitment to Welfare*. New York: Random House.

Tonelson, Alan. 2000. *The Race to the Bottom*. Boulder, CO: Westview Press.

Uzzi, Brian. 1997. "Social Structure and Competition in Interfirm Networks: The Paradox of Embeddedness." *Administrative Science Quarterly* 42:35–67.

Verba, Sidney, Kay Lehman Schlozman, and Henry Brady. 1996. *Voice and Equality: Civic Voluntarism in American Politics*. Cambridge: Harvard University Press.

Visser, Jelle. 1996. *Unionisation Trends. The OECD Countries Union Membership File*. Amsterdam: University of Amsterdam, Centre for Research of European Societies and Labour Relations.

Wallerstein, Michael, and Bruce Western. 2000. "Unions in Decline? What Has Changed and Why." *Annual Review of Political Science* 3:355–377.

Warner, Stephen. 1993. "Work in Progress toward a New Paradigm for the Sociological Study of Religion in the United States." *American Journal of Sociology* 98:1044–93.

Weaver, R. Kent. 2000. *Ending Welfare as We Know It*. Washington, DC: Brookings Institution Press.

Weir, Margaret, Ann Orloff, and Theda Skocpol. 1988a. "Introduction: Understanding American Social Politics." In *The Politics of Social Policy in the United States*.

Edited by Margaret Weir, Ann Orloff, and Theda Skocpol, 3–27. Princeton: Princeton University Press.

————. 1988b. *The Politics of Social Policy in the United States.* Princeton, NJ: Princeton University Press.

Wildavsky, Aaron. 1987. "Choosing Preferences by Constructing Institutions: A Cultural Theory of Preference Formation." *American Political Science Review* 81:3–22.

Wilensky, Harold. 1965. *Industrial Society and Social Welfare: The Impact of Industrialization on the Supply and Organization of Social Welfare Services in the United States.* New York: Free Press.

————. 1975. *The Welfare State and Equality.* Berkeley: University of California Press.

————. 2002. *Rich Democracies: Political Economy, Public, and Performance.* Berkeley: University of California Press.

Wlezien, Christopher. 1995. "The Public as Thermostat: Dynamics of Preferences for Spending." *American Journal of Political Science* 39:981–1000.

————. 1996. "Dynamics of Representation: The Case of US Spending on Defence." *British Journal of Political Science* 26: 81–103.

————. 2004. "Patterns of Representation: Dynamics of Public Preferences and Policy." *Journal of Politics* 66:1–24.

Wlezien, Christopher, and Soroka, Stuart. 2003. "Measures and Models of Budgetary Policy." *Policy Studies Journal* 31:273–86.

Wooldridge, Jeffrey. 2002. *Econometric Analysis of Cross Section and Panel Data.* Cambridge: MIT Press.

Woodberry, Robert, and Christian Smith. 1998. "Fundamentalism et al.: Conservative Protestants in America." *Annual Review of Sociology* 24:25–56.

Wright, Erik Olin. 1994. *Interrogating Inequality: Essays on Class Analysis, Socialism, and Marxism.* London: Verso.

Wuthnow, Robert. 1988. *The Restructuring of American Religion: Society and Faith since World War II.* Princeton, NJ: Princeton University Press.

Zaller, John. 1992. *The Nature and Origin of Mass Opinion.* New York: Cambridge University Press.

Zerubavel, Eviatar. 2003. *Time Maps: Collective Memory and the Social Shape of the Past.* Chicago: University of Chicago Press.

Index